29 Rules for Smart Parenting

29 Rules for Smart Parenting

How to Raise Children without Being a Tyrant

Rolf Arnold

ROWMAN & LITTLEFIELD

Lanham • Boulder • New York • London

Published by Rowman & Littlefield
A wholly owned subsidary of The Rowman & Littlefield Publishing Group, Inc.
4501 Forbes Boulevard, Suite 200, Lanham, Maryland 20706
www.rowman.com

Unit A, Whitacre Mews, 26-34 Stannary Street, London SE11 4AB

Translated from the original German by Glenn M. Peach

British Library Cataloguing in Publication Information Available

Library of Congress Cataloging-in-Publication Data Available

Arnold, Rolf, 1952- author.
29 rules for smart parenting : how to raise children without being a tyrant / Rolf Arnold.
    pages cm
Includes bibliographical references.
ISBN 978-1-4758-1471-2 (cloth : alk. paper) — ISBN 978-1-4758-2156-7 (pbk.) — ISBN 978-1-4758-1472-9 (electronic) 1. Parenting. 2. Parent and child. 3. Teaching. 4. Teacher-student relationships. I. Title. II. Title: Twenty nine rules for smart parenting.
HQ755.8.A726 2015
306.874—dc23   2015024411

∞™ The paper used in this publication meets the minimum requirements of American National Standard for Information Sciences—Permanence of Paper for Printed Library Materials, ANSI/NISO Z39.48-1992.

Printed in the United States of America

"It's no good hoping one day
your children will be little angels,
but you can do something that
helps you to become a better parent."
(Dreikurs 2010, p. 22)

Contents

Preface

Textbox P.1

The following situation took place in a streetcar in Zurich:

Four youths got into a streetcar and, talking loudly among themselves, occupied several of the available seats. At the next stop, an elderly couple boarded the car and the man addressed one of the youths with the hopeful request, "Would you let my wife sit down please? She is not feeling well!" The youth, apparently hearing this as an interruption of his conversation, looked menacingly back at the man and said, "Then tell her to stay at home. I am sick too—sick of school," causing the rest of the group to break out in a roar of laughter. Another elderly woman, who had observed the situation, stood up and offered her seat to the woman. The man acknowledged her kind action and muttered something like "Today's youth has no upbringing." The woman nodded and moved to the rear of the car.

Similar situations can be observed every day of the week. According to the German weekly news periodical *Focus*, 54 percent of the German mothers feel overwhelmed by the duties of raising children.[1] At the same time, still in broad circulation is the old complaint that child rearing used to be different and certainly seemed so much better back in time. Even in ancient times, Socrates lamented about the spoiled youth. Sometimes, the complaint is accompanied by explicit demands "to do something about it"—but what?

Parents and teachers are confronted with accusations of lacking the courage to educate and, therefore, share responsibility for what is decried as rudeness, slackness, decadence, or even neglect of "the youth today." All too often, the ensuing response consists of resolutions calling for a "crackdown" and demands like "Don't let them get away with that" or "Exert your authority."

As a result, students are repeatedly sent to the principal's office; in other cases, voices are raised and the lecturing begins, and so forth. In the end, as parents and teachers, we have an arsenal of *stopgap measures* at our disposal, although the more we use them, the less we are convinced of their effectiveness. In such situations, it is our guts that do the talking, not our heads, and certainly not our hearts. Even educational research often fails to deliver on its promises when it comes to everyday parenting situations. We are left with the only available conclusion: *"Education is necessary, but impossible."*

This sobering assessment is not meant to imply that research has not found anything that might help a father, a mother, or a teacher to know what to do or, perhaps, what is better left undone. However, the findings are varied and they do not lend themselves to simple rules that would tell us which paths lead to success and which do not. Consequently, as worried parents and teachers, we are initially well advised to say good-bye to all of the simple models—those with the motto "Come on, try . . ."—and instead, bring yourself to understand what parenting means and why it is often so difficult to really achieve the permanent behavioral changes that you would like to see in your child. This idea of "permanent" is what poses the real problem because determined explanations, firm warnings, and strict disciplinary measures usually only produce a short-term behavioral modification—behavior that is socially desirable or forced, but in most cases, not grounded on internal conviction. Therefore, these determined parenting measures are accompanied by risk and side effects, for which abundant evidence exists in the files of the child psychologists and family therapists. Nevertheless, we tend to rely on these risky practices over and over again—out of helplessness and, not infrequently, from overwork, or even anger and disappointment. Why is it that we so often turn to old-fashioned thinking and actions in matters of parenting?

It is our unique childhood and adolescent experiences that provide us with our stock of "parenting tools," according to the technical terminology of pedagogy.

In stressful situations, how we were treated in our youth determines the way we act. We are moved in similar situations by the deep emotions of our own suffering to act in a similar manner, just with the poles reversed. Parenting practices are passed on from generation to generation and it takes a consequential decision to step away from

Textbox P.2

A teacher working with us in the context of support for a conflict resolution told us this: "Petra reminds me of myself so much. I was also so annoying to my surroundings and was constantly provoking my parents. They were not amused and reacted rather aggressively: I had 'house arrest' for the whole summer while my friends were allowed to do all kinds of things. There was also corporal punishment and I developed a very negative self-image: 'You'll never make it!'—was one of the most common expressions heard around my house. Or, the constant accusation: 'After all we have done for you, how can you be so ungrateful?' Actually, I can only remember my mother saying such things. Shocked, I notice myself again and again making similar accusations against Petra, whose integration in the classroom receives more of my attention than other children. However, the more I try, the more she interrupts my class. This makes me angry and I catch myself over and over again responding with draconian punishments, instead of seeking a real dialog."

this and to create a different educational universe for your children or students.

The past shapes us, but sometimes paralyzes us too. In educational conflict situations, we often repeat what we know because only that, and no other way, is what we experienced ourselves or observed in others. At the foreground is always our sense of what we think is appropriate, anything else is hard to accept. We react, because from somewhere deep down inside, the behavior appears to us as unacceptable, this or that simply cannot stand. Uncomprehending, we can only shake our head when the educational advisor tells us we should try to not react. "But that just doesn't work!"—screams out every cell of our body, and still the doubt lingers when we find that the educational responses we make have ended again with no effect.

Our more thoughtful inner advisor checks in with us from time to time in the quiet moments: "What are you trying to achieve? Would you like to feel better about yourself in the short term because you did something, or do you want to help your child develop more and more appropriate forms of behavior?" We have to admit, "Yes, that is it. What we really want is for our child to behave independently more and more in the way we expect." While we are saying this, we notice in parallel how contradictory that is: "Figure it out on your own" and "behave in the manner expected." How is that supposed to happen? Doesn't this expectation lead down the same dead-end path? Just like the road educational science calls "the road to *intentional* education"?

For many centuries, pedagogy was based on the assumption that *clarity of purpose* was the main condition for a successful education. It was assumed that after you have a clearly defined direction in which you want to teach, all the necessities would be taken care of, and you only had to apply the appropriate teaching measures such as rewards, punishment, or affection. This assumption has often ended in disappointment. Over and over, we are forced to acknowledge that the impact of all our efforts to achieve the clear educational goals is always uncertain or without conviction. What is true in our attempts at persuasion is also true in our parenting attempts: some people can be convinced, others cannot be. Some people can be very persuasive and others cannot be.

> *When asking ourselves how we can be more effective as parents, we must also consider how convincing we are as educators. Do we reach for our teaching tools thoughtlessly, impulsively, or just routinely and simply start teaching? Or, do we wonder: "Is the other person following any of this?"*

If we could look into the hearts and minds of our children, we would often realize how little contact there is when we are teaching them. Many may be afraid when they are thinking "Here he goes again, another heart attack!" and they let it pass right over them, and the parents never really get in touch with the child through the response they have made. Such parenting is destined to fail before it even begins, because the contact between the participants was broken off long ago. Parents and teachers then find themselves in a situation where they are trying to convince someone of something while the other person has stopped listening several minutes ago. The persuader can repeat the argument over and over and talk even louder, but no real feedback from the counterparty can be expected.

The key question regarding the effectiveness of child rearing is a much earlier one: Are you (still) in touch with your child (or your student)? *This is the reason why all effective teaching measures focus, at their core, on shaping the relationship.* Teaching without a relationship is like swimming without water! This means you cannot raise a child well if there is no real relationship. Of course, it is all about the kind of relationship which you, as the adult, establish towards your children. This is not a partnership and our children are not our friends—they are something else and more: they need our adult voice, but also our affection and guidance—in a positive, that is, horizon-broadening, security-giving, and also a boundary-marking way.

> *A true relationship is always characterized by an interest in the development and growth of the other person. Parenting goes further than this and is based on a loving responsibility for the development of a child.*

On this basis, any advice to establish a friendly relationship with your children misses the fundamental point in the parenting challenge: the responsibility felt and lived. This provides a feeling of security that is far different from feeling accepted in a friendly relationship. Children realize, in this elevated awareness, that something is expected of them, but at the same time, also know they are on "safe ground" to experiment, to try, and to fail. Such parenting builds trust and establishes an inner basis on which self-confidence and personal responsibility can develop and mature.

Textbox P.3

> "It was always very important to me," one mother said, "for our children to stand on a different level. You may not believe it, but I was never an advocate of the parent-child partnership. It has been my experience that children draw a lot of confidence from the fact that we as adults play a special role for them, with special concerns and issues that we do not have to discuss with them. Only with clear lines of separation, can children attend to their own task: self-effort and self-development. Those educators—like many of my friends—who treat children as adults harm the child as well as themselves. Children are and remain children, even if you give them room to discuss or even to decide, but often they may appear fully inflated, but are not really satisfied. Parents just hurt themselves by such blurring of the lines."

This book is about the concept of inclusive parenting and teaching. The 29 rules for smart parenting are intended to help the reader in becoming more effective as parents and teachers.

NOTE

1. *Focus*, February 21, 2009, p. 81.

When you feel your child or adolescent is "difficult," before reacting out of anger or disappointment, go back to the source of your love!

Children and teenagers are still developing. They are discovering themselves. They can do this if they are able to find/define "definitions" of their own. The word "definition" already includes the root topic. It is all about boundaries (Latin: *finis*, the boundary).

Children do not "need" boundaries, as some parenting books conclusively advise—much more, they "seek" boundaries.

Many problems in child rearing are the result of attempting to find these boundaries. Children and teenagers present themselves anew to us. They depart from the old, no longer wanting to be a child and we often perceive their behavior as impudent or even pretentious, egotistical or even outrageous. Our parenting reactions are then controlled by our emotions (disappointment, anger, frustration, etc.). Not infrequently, we then try to impose our own ideas, completely overlooking the fact that we are also trying to hold onto something that has already slipped out of our grasp.

Textbox 1.1

A mother described to me in despair her frustration and anger: "For some time now, my son has been acting contrary to everything I hold dear: He does not care about the family, takes everything for granted, leaves his room a total mess, and reacts aggressively if I point this out to him. I think I have failed miserably as a parent."

When such disappointment overwhelms us and generates negative thoughts within us, the only thing we can do is return to the source of our love for the other person. This is the place where we, as parents or teachers unconditionally say "yes" to the child's searching and development. Nevertheless, our own needs and expectations must also be expressed without reproach. After the rules are set, let them know there is a price to pay if these are broken and show them that this will be enforced. This is a three-step approach to open and consequential parenting, one which accepts changes in our children.

CLEAR AND CONSEQUENTIAL PARENTING

Love, clarity, and consistency are the three essential pillars of successful parenting. However, this does not imply that their presence is a guarantee of success in every case. Parenting is far more uncertain and insecure in its outcome. Nevertheless, we have determined that in the absence of these three pillars, no real and lasting educational effects can be produced. This applies to the relationship between parents and their children, as well as between teachers and their students, who not only provide instruction but also teach their students. Often, teaching is what establishes the basis for the subsequent successful instruction. It does not help to complain that "today's children have no upbringing" or that they receive too little discipline at home, and schools are overburdened trying to balance the mistakes of the family. Yearning for "love" is also a futile exercise as it is something we cannot expect from a "stranger's kids."

Table 1.1

Three steps to clear and consequential parenting	
Feel the love	Enjoy the calm feeling that comes over you when you see your child. Enjoy watching their struggles, their efforts to discover and find themselves!
Let go of the expectations	Focus your inner eye on the blank canvas, where your child is painting their own future! Imagine how surprising and different this will be. Different from everything you thought you knew.
Specify the price	Define five key rules of behavior and cooperation! Write down a kind of "catalog of fines" and hang it in a common area. This is effective only if you enforce it.

Such argumentation overlooks the fact that teaching and parenting are two paths to the same goal: *to form the next generation of a society into mature, helpful, and knowledgeable adults.* Professionals in child and adolescent development (teachers) have an important role. We expect them not to surrender in the face of difficulties, but rather to remain professional and wait for them to show us clear forms of support, so our children can "find themselves." In doing this, they remind us that this search has always been difficult and rough. They must also be aware that in today's complex world with its multicultural and accelerated contexts, the job of an educator is getting even more difficult.

STAY IN TOUCH

The important question for parents and teachers as to the effectiveness of parenting is this: Are you (still) in touch with your children/students?

The checklist below will help you perform a quick self-assessment of whether or not you are truly in touch with your child or student. Please be quick and spontaneous in your answers.

If you have answered more than five of these questions with "Sometimes" or "Never," you should seek to improve the contact with your child or student, by learning how to deliberately reach out to them. The other rules for smart parenting provide tips and advice on how you can do this.

Checklist: How effective is my teaching/parenting?			
Self-assessment questions:	Often	Sometimes	Never
(1) I know what currently concerns my child/student and what they are feeling.			
(2) I initiate "you-are-important" actions, oriented on the actual desires of the other party.			
(3) I always talk with my child/student—in a way that ensures the talk is not a one-sided conversation.			
(4) I encourage, praise, and value much more often than I warn and rebuke.			
(5) I control my own attitudes, emotions, and disappointments and never take it out on my children/students.			
(6) If my child/student comes to me, I always give them my devoted attention in a friendly and unhurried manner.			
(7) I can forgive and never hold a grudge or insist on an explanation or an excuse.			
(8) My child/student asks me for advice.			
(9) I trust my children/students and have confidence in them.			
(10) I never break off the contact to my children/students and I notice when they are withdrawn.			

Figure 1.1

When confronted with violence— show no fear. Meet and defuse it by projecting a controlled presence!

We hear more and more complaints, in particular from teachers, about the violence and aggression in children and teenagers. Brawls on the playground are among the harmless expressions of this violence and, although it costs money, the destruction in the restrooms or classrooms is at least repairable. But the prevalence of gangs, extortion, and coercion among students can take on a cruel dimension and affect the developmental opportunities of the child or adolescent or even lead to serious traumatization.

> Teachers must not look the other way. On the contrary, they should watch out for such situations, confront the parties involved, and stop the violent acts. Punishment is at best an effective deterrent, and then, only over the short term. Rather, the parties must be confronted with their violent behavior and be exposed to other forms of conflict resolution.

SOMETIMES FAMILIES NEED HELP

Situations appear now and again in families where the parents are no longer able to stand up to their child. Time and again, we hear about situations in which sons hit their mothers and torment or even terrorize their younger siblings. In such situations, the family needs help and support. Teachers who suspect or become aware of such conditions in the family have the duty to intervene. The first step may be a visit to the family for a caring conversation with one or both of the parents. It may be appropriate to offer the assistance of child care services or educational counseling that could be made available. In particularly difficult cases, socio-educational support is to be considered, where the child is taken away from the family to special youth camps (usually abroad) for a short time to relearn, step by step, the basic forms of living together. In any case, the rule is this: silence encourages the continuation of violence and violence always causes injury, illness, and pain for others.

CHILDREN OFTEN NEED HELP

Parents often lament that their response is limited to the attempt to prevent youth violence directed against each other, or even towards parents or teachers—a process of punishing extreme versions of insubordinate behavior.

For all our revulsion over violent acts, we must not overlook the fact that it is precisely those who resort to force that need our help, support, and attention the most. They are not "bad by nature," but rather, have never experienced in their development any positive example for nonviolent forms of conflict resolution.

The assessment "every violent juvenile offender has experienced violence firsthand" is certainly too general; nevertheless, numerous studies support this belief. Those who turn to violence have had to endure it themselves as a "reliable" form of behavior. It represents a familiar pattern of behavior for them. Teachers, in particular, are not only expected to put an end to violent situations; they must also turn to the offenders with special offers. The common effect of exclusion and rejection as part of the punishment especially, then, is that the offender will again engage in violence. In this way, they are assured of attracting attention.

Not to be underestimated is the fact that children often experience violence at home. Experienced educators and teachers can often feel this in the overly anxious behavior of these children and it is not unusual that bruises, welts, or injuries can also tell a clear story. The German Child Protection Agency (*Kinderschutzbund*) regularly publishes statistics that show how widespread the mistreatment or even abuse in the family really is. Every day children have their souls broken under the guise of parental authority—an incompatible state of affairs in a society that prides itself on humanity and development support.

To look away is to prolong the suffering of these children. Your interference is demanded because educators are also advocates for the well-being of the child. The authority of parents finds its limit at the point where it degenerates into physical violence.

WHAT CAN BE DONE?

As parents and educators we must train ourselves to act immediately to prevent overt violence and to uncover latent violence and make it manageable.

All violent behavior that we are able to see and access in order to intervene is overt. In contrast, latent violence refers to the more subtle forms of cruelty among schoolchildren or to the endured acts of domestic violence.

Table 2.1

How to deal with violent behavior	Course of action
Prevention of overt violence	Intervene without hesitation ("I am in charge here!")
	Use a firm voice and determined presence ("I will not tolerate violent behavior!")
The aim is to effect an immediate end to the violence.	Master your own fear ("I will not be intimidated!")
Exposing latent violence	Seek facts, investigate, and use direct questioning ("This is a matter of concern to me!")
	Possibly confront and make it public ("This is wrong and harmful!")
The aim is to break down the wall of silence.	Shine a light into the darkness ("Let the latent become overt!")

Dealing with both forms of violence requires courage and determination. It is much easier to look away. But that results in permanent harm to the young people—often with an irreparable damage to the soul of the individual and to the social environment. Children and teenagers can learn peaceful forms of conflict resolution only when violence is outlawed and when it can no longer be tolerated.

As parents and educators deal a defeat to violence, they make a major contribution to the emergence of a peaceful society. Nonviolent education, with bold and decisive action against all forms of violence, provides a valuable experience for children and teenagers. They can see for themselves that there are people who do not give violent behavior a chance and who even practice nonviolent forms of conflict resolution. This is the fundamental basis of humanity and democracy.

If you can avoid the use of violence and oppose all forms of violent behavior, you will educate the child more than you can imagine. By letting them observe and experience nonviolent forms of cooperation and conflict resolution, you are giving the only gift we have for raising kind people.

If you feel the need to impose sanctions or punishment, first perform a "culpability" check. Keep the level of punishment low in relation to the damages suffered!

There may be situations in which children or teenagers are the cause of serious damage. Perhaps, they break a valuable object, or they cause a traffic situation that results in claims for damages, or they seriously insult or maybe even slander someone. Such situations demand a disciplinary action. An important prerequisite for imposing a successful sanction, however, is to give a prudent response, not an immediate reaction. What do we mean by this?

Every sanction should have a substantive relevance to the damage. In other words, whoever breaks a window should help to pay for a new window. Whoever offends someone should apologize to the victim or be encouraged to show that person that they regret the behavior.

Textbox 3.1

Disciplinary sanctions are consequences that must be expected and accepted by the one who caused the damage. The basis of every sanction is this: The sanction must have a substantive relevance to the damage.

"Please try that with my oldest one. He will just spit at you," said one frustrated Mom when I tried to explain the principles of effective disciplinary sanctions. "He will not do what I tell him. It is all the same to him. When I then try to reason with him, he explodes. Let me tell you: the only thing that helps at that point is the old-fashioned method: No allowance money, house arrest, and a good chewing out." When asked

what the use of these old methods has achieved in the past, the mother had no answer. Helplessly, she added "But you have to do something; you can't just let it go."

Just "letting it go" is not an alternative, neither is the repeated use of sanctions that you already know will not have a lasting effect. There are three questions we must ask ourselves if the goal is to find an effective sanction:

- What sanction is appropriate and realistic in its substance?
- Can I actually implement this punishment?
- How can I lend credence to my sanction?

WHAT SANCTION IS APPROPRIATE AND REALISTIC?

Teachers and parents often raise the level when deciding on a punishment. For example, the punishment for disobedience or impudence is detention, or pocket money is withheld for arriving home too late. Although unpleasant or even painful for the child, such punishments are of little effect—because nothing is learned, except for experiencing punishment as unpleasant. To make matters worse: a genuine teaching opportunity is wasted.

Before reacting, take the time to consider: What is an appropriate and realistic disciplinary response?

Let me suggest that it is more effective to punish getting home late by shortening the usual play time by one hour. The child learns the habit of checking his watch. Only if this does not bring the desired result, is it time to consider a period of detention. It is clearly helpful to praise improved behavior without directly canceling the punishment. If the punishment imposed is understood as "So, for the next week you have to be home before 9:00 p.m.!" you should not change it just because the deadline is being met two days in a row. But, you may certainly say, "I see that you are learning to be on time now!"

CAN I ACTUALLY IMPLEMENT THIS PUNISHMENT?

Our educational effort has little chance of success if we try to impose a sanction that we know we cannot, or will not, ever implement. In this case, it is always a good practice to develop graduated levels of response and not threaten the final level right from the start. If we respond directly with a period of detention, we forfeit other possibilities. The children do not get the chance to prove themselves in order to avoid the more extreme punishments.

In principle, only impose sanctions that, if not fulfilled, can be expressed even more clearly. Parents and educators who use their full supply of power in their immediate reaction have nothing left in reserve. What can they do if the desired behavior is not forthcoming or the ban is ignored?

The educational response in terms of its demands or severity should always stay below the damage suffered or inflicted. It is not true that draconian punishments are the best guarantee that the sanctioned behavior will never again be repeated. Draconian punishments mainly damage and humiliate the offender, often leaving behind a frustration that promotes aggression. From an educational perspective, the major lesson to take away in the area of sanctions is to provide a learning experience that shows damage can always be repaired.

HOW CAN I LEND CREDENCE TO MY SANCTION?

Reinforcement is only possible when you, as the responsible educator, still have further sanctions available, but this carries a great escalation risk (motto: "If you don't, then . . .!"). This is why it is so important when in the midst of conflict situation, for example, after having just imposed a punishment, to avoid any implication that you will love the child again only if he or she is obedient. An atmosphere of conditionality must be avoided at all cost.

On the contrary, if you have confronted your child with a punishment, it is best to leave it at that. It is important at this point to treat your child with love and as a friend. This will help the child to accept the punishment without bitterness or anger. The words "So, that is the way I expect it to be from now on and with that the incident is over for me!" must be said out loud so that—at another level—the relationship can continue. In the parenting conflict, the responsible educator has the difficult task of maintaining a relationship with the child and "leaving it at that."

THE FIVE FINGER CHECK

Perform a five finger check before you choose and announce the punishment. If you answer "no" to any of the questions in the checklist, it is an indication that you must thoroughly reconsider and plan your response. Remember, never act on a gut feeling alone and never resort to physical punishment!

The Five Finger Check: The Art of Effective Disciplinary Actions		Yes	No
1.	Is the damage the result of carelessness, recklessness, or intent?		
2.	Have I considered the context of the damage in forming my reaction (to cause concern and anxiety in others is also an injury)		
3.	Do I have a set of graduated responses, so I can start with the first level?		
4.	Have I kept my educational response to a level below the degree of damage suffered or inflicted?		
5.	Have I ensured that my reaction will not end my relationship with the child and I can "leave it at that"?		

Figure 3.1

Live by the values you want your
child to be committed to in life!

The values question is a perennial favorite in the teaching debate. Especially when some unthinkable, monstrous event happens and the press, radio, and TV reports outbid one another with different demands of what should be done. The most popular of these is to demand a severe response and seek to make an example as a warning to others. These ideas thrive on the unproven assumption that children and teenagers must be forced into good behavior. Such loud claims hide the more thoughtful reactions, those that would remind us that each adult generation throughout history has had a problem or even been angered with the behavior of the younger generation. This is documented in records extending way back to ancient times.

What is sometimes overlooked is the fact that we, as educators, seldom encounter those extreme situations so eagerly reported in the media. Rarely do we meet a parent or teacher that has personally experienced gangs, violent assaults, and other criminal acts. Nevertheless, such extreme situations often come to define our picture of the next generation and we catch ourselves thinking that behind every jostle or rude behavior is a potential act of violence. Such extremism in educational thinking does more harm than good. If we attempt to focus our entire educational concept on the prevention of juvenile delinquency, we lose touch with reality and we lack ideas and no longer know what to do.

The reality for our children—as in all the preceding centuries of human development—is their attempt to set themselves apart and test their own standards of thinking, feeling, and acting. In these times, it is surely not easy for us to support this search but, in most cases, it is still true that education will prevail.

A father reported, in his words, the "extreme forms of behavior" his son began to take on in terms of the nature of his clothes and his circle of "strange" friends. "In his way of thinking, he is really hurting all the things I hold to be important. He cares only for himself and the family home is nothing but a hotel for him! In all honesty, I hate to say it, but he has become really unpleasant. If I didn't know he was my son, I would avoid all dealings with him."

How can we get our children or our students to orient their thoughts, feelings, and actions on what we consider to be basic humanitarian or socially appropriate behavior? This is the question that has always concerned and motivated parents. It is possible in strictly controlled societies, or those of a militaristic nature, to achieve the desired behavior through draconian punishments. This method cannot be the goal of a democratic society.

We must first admit that it is not possible for us to force our children and teenagers to follow the same values that we have chosen for ourselves. On the contrary, they must set themselves apart if they are to discover the values on which they will base their own thoughts, feelings, and actions as individuals. This insight is not widely shared. First, we have to ask ourselves the following questions:

Are you prepared to let your children or students search entirely on their own and in experimental ways? What "extreme forms" of self-expression are you willing to tolerate? Or, (more fundamentally asked): Is it really important to you that your child discovers his own basic values for life? If so, you must accept the fact that the child can only succeed if allowed to follow his own individual way.

VISIBLE COMMITMENT TO VALUES

Parents and educators can support them along their way by visibly living the values. This means expressing over and over again the "rules" of respect, courtesy to others, and serious dialog when dealing with counterparts in an educational exchange. This is not easy and failures are frequent because we are sometimes at a loss or maybe even angry. But values are never transferred or even taught, they must be experienced. The fundamental questions to be asked by the responsible educator are:

- What are the values in your life?
- Are you loyal to these values?
- How is your commitment to these values visible to others such as your children?
- Is your values message sometimes weakened by actions that are different from the way you think or feel or behave?

If you want education to impart values, then you must first be aware of your own values. Your expectations for your children's behavior should not be shouted at but, rather, lived. For many parents and educators this message is both provocative and, certainly, worthwhile. If we think about the questions raised earlier, we find over and over again that we start to deal differently with children and adolescents and that this different response produces different results.

Let your values shine through in the way you live. Consider this: values cannot be taught—they can only be experienced and sensed.

Often, we repeatedly insist on summoning our own values from others. But in some cases, that is how we destroy exactly those values that we are trying to express. Let's be clear about the fact that what children and teenagers experience is what determines, in their own way, how they differentiate themselves in order to become an individual.

EMPHASIZE INDIRECT METHODS

There is a strong consensus in the so-called moral education that strongly favors an indirect teaching method. The indirect method ensures that children and teenagers can experience what it is (we are) about. This method includes, for example, the approaches shown below:

- Children and teenagers learn classic democratic principles by experiencing the democratic rules of the game in the schools and at home. By experiencing such embryonic democracy, they develop a capacity for democratic values. By confronting them with gruff authority, we are only inviting them to return gruff patterns of behavior.
- Children and teenagers are more likely to choose nonviolent forms of communication and conflict resolution when they have experienced and practiced similar forms in their daily lives.
- You can treat dissident thinkers or different ideas with respect and in a worthy manner only if you have personally experienced such treatment when you are the one who is different—being the minority or less experienced.
- Appreciation, respect, and friendliness can develop fully only if children and teenagers experience them constantly, especially in their "extreme" searching phases.

Remember: The behaviors of children and teenagers often follow precisely the subtle messages that we expect from them.

Don't just give an adequate response, have quid pro quo exchanges!

There are many times when we are confronted with a form of behavior where we clearly say to ourselves: "This cannot just pass by so easily!" In such situations, we often let a spontaneous reaction take over. "Rudeness must be answered with rudeness!" is just one of the slogans that come to mind once again as we confirm—in our own mind—that our response is fully justified. We become loud, randomly choose a punishment—aimed at a tender spot sometimes—and we have inner dialogs to justify our indignation: "Who does he think he is!" "I will not be treated in this way!" "I will show him where the boundaries are!" All are emotional forms of response stemming from our own feelings of being offended or even having been angered, which have very little to do with the offender but tell us a lot about ourselves.

Textbox 5.1

The following scene was played out at a vocational school in Rhineland-Palatinate: Daniel once again came late to class and chose this time a particularly flashy form of entry. He swung open the classroom door, clicked his heels together, and gave the Hitler salute! The young and very dedicated social studies teacher was visibly shocked, the class cheered. Daniel crashed down into his seat and leaned back casually. The teacher responded in a decisive manner: he briefed the principal, Daniel was suspended from school for two weeks and his parents were summoned for an interview. All hell broke loose at home: Daniel's father took away his motor scooter

(cont...)

Textbox 5.1 *(cont...)*

and refused to speak another word with his wayward son. He was deeply ashamed. The young social studies teacher seized the opportunity to incorporate an impromptu series of lessons about National Socialism in his curriculum.

What do the educational responses of the principal, the father, and the teacher tell us?

From a moral point of view, we might be able to understand this decisiveness and may even agree with it, but not from an educational standpoint. Before judging the effectiveness of a teaching measure, we have to always ask ourselves how it could be perceived in the world of the person at whom it is directed. It is important to ask especially in such "difficult cases": What do we know about Daniel's situation? Why did he turn to such "extreme" forms of expression?

THE WORLD OF THE "AT-RISK" CHILD

This term refers, in child development research, to teenagers who tend towards a radical, right-wing worldview, violent assaults against foreigners, or conformism into right-wing extremist groups. Research studies about these youths clearly show us that it almost always involves young people that

- have problems in school,
- feel unwelcome in their own home,
- have rarely experienced self-pride, and
- have been unable, in the past, to develop anything more than a relatively weak self-confidence.

For this reason, the "promises" and the "experienced" world represented by right-wing extremist groups appear as solutions in the eyes of such teenagers:

- They no longer feel like losers, because it is enough to be "German" and know that "Our time will come!"
- They no longer feel alone and unwelcomed. They find camaraderie at the campfire and in a world of simple slogans, blame, and common enemies.
- They can experience self-efficacy through common group activities (such as violently attacking minorities).
- They receive a picture they can identify with (who they are).

The at-risk teenagers are attracted to a right-wing extremist group because the group offers suitable solutions to their problems. Some teenagers are unable to see for themselves how inappropriate and dangerous such solutions are. These youths will be socially isolated and will not find what they are actually searching for—namely, a place in society—because to them, in the past, society has been a fragile and threatening thing. Such experiences are reinforced by the actions of the administrators, teachers, and parents, as in the case above. Once again, Daniel is isolated and learns that he does not belong in the society, and again, he is greeted with the familiar words, "There is something wrong with you!" Only with a thorough analysis of Daniel's life do we realize that through his "extreme behavior," he has once again "picked up" exactly *that* experience, which—unconsciously—perpetuates his isolation. A fundamental rule applies:

> An educational response always requires that you first ask yourself what the offender is expressing with the "extreme" behavior. Avoid reactions that may, in effect, serve to confirm the world experienced by the teenager and validate his initial threatening experience. Otherwise, you may—unintentionally—end up affirming what you mean to disapprove.

A professional educational response, therefore, must be concerned with preventing such counter effects. This requires you to consider how the world is experienced by the teenager and how he or she feels and finds his or her way. With this insight, one can develop educational responses that actually have a chance of working. Specifically, parents and educators should ask themselves if their response will produce another experience in which the disturbed youth(s) feel(s) once again like failure(s), unwelcomed, or self-ineffectual.

Educational responses should aim precisely at what the teenager is so vehemently demanding with the extreme behavior. *Effective education is not achieved by reacting out of anger; rather, your response should be decided after decrypting the offending behavior.* Of course, this does not imply that parents or educators should never express anger or, sometimes, even react rashly. The key is to manage the exceptional teenager with a view to the medium and long term: Is their behavior resentful, immobilizing, and exclusionary? Are they capable of responding effectively, in a way that is in keeping with the life experiences of the other person? This is the so-called "principle of equivalence" in effective parenting:

> Ensure that your reation always creates a resonance and develops perspectives in the world of the offender!

In our specific example, after the incident occurred, the teacher did not immediately approach Daniel; rather he kept this teenager in mind as a "special" case and modified his future dealings with him:

Textbox 5.2

In the subsequent weeks and months, the teacher made an effort to address Daniel directly and integrate him into the class' social activities. Daniel was taken aback when the teacher chose him to assist in the planning of the next class trip. The teacher entrusted him with this responsibility and Daniel had the chance to report every two weeks the details to the class and even involve others in the planning preparations. The teacher took every opportunity to praise Daniel for his contribution and even awarded him public recognition—in class. Initially, Daniel appeared to be overwhelmed and there were times and situations where he seemed to be seeking an excuse to quit and return to his familiar world of "I do not belong here." After some time, however, he grew into the challenge and finished the job to everyone's satisfaction.

Always look for the impression behind the expression!

Children and teenagers often pass through unstable phases in the search for themselves and sometimes resort to harsh expressions. Many parents no longer recognize their sons and daughters during this phase: the friendly and optimistic child they knew has become an egotistical and unfriendly teenager who now treats everything with indifference, no matter what the parents expect.

Textbox 6.1

"Well to be perfectly honest," said one father during a parent counseling session, "I have to say that my son is a real disappointment. He just takes, never thinks of others, and even fills his leisure time mostly with consumption and, more recently, partying and alcohol. He seems oblivious to what we parents think. Actually, it is more like the opposite: the more he notices our dissatisfaction, the more extreme his behavior becomes. You should see what he runs around in. I refuse to be seen with him any longer; what must the people think?"

Such disappointment on the part of parents and responsible educators is the reason why they are so often tempted to speak harshly and give the youth "a piece of their mind" (even when the youths have already known for quite some time that we disapprove of, and even reject, their appearance and/or their behavior). Nevertheless, they continue to provoke us. And what do we do? We let ourselves be provoked and react to the provocation—not to what the child is searching for through this form of expression. The original meaning of the Latin root word for "provoke" is "to call forth." The question is, what are the children and teenagers trying to "call forth" when they break the rules or don't meet our expectations? Try to see what is really behind their "expressions."

Textbox 6.2

At a teacher's conference, while discussing the expulsion of a "difficult" student, who made personal insults to the teaching staff and annoyed the classes with his loud and provocative behavior, one of the teachers surprised all those present with the comment: "Well, you must admit that what Johnny has done is quite an achievement. Just consider what it means to have occupied the entire teaching staff for nearly two hours in a discussion just about him. I was never able to do that as a child. My impression is that we are doing precisely what Johnny wants us to do. OK, so maybe he has not found the proper form of expression to call attention to himself. But, isn't that just what this is all about? He is saying to us: 'Deal with me: I need some reaction from you to acknowledge that I exist!' And what are we doing now? We are doing his bidding, by busying ourselves now with thoughts of a properly spectacular reaction." "What crap," said one colleague who particularly suffered under Johnny's provocations. "What do you suggest? Do nothing and let everything just continue to happen? Surely, you cannot be serious!"

LOOK FOR THE BACKGROUND

In the subsequent heated debate, the teacher was able to convince her colleagues that more attention be focused on the impression that Johnny has of his own situation. Only then could they succeed in reaching an educational response that is not influenced by their own indignation, but rather refers directly to the actual case.

The search for the impression behind the expression is the basic step towards an effective educational reaction. The key question is: What do we know about the views of the "provocateur"? Or, how does life feel in the place where the student is positioned?

This way of dealing with the impression behind the expression corresponds to the manner employed, for example, by doctors and other charitable professions. They do not react until they have a detailed analysis of the symptoms; moreover, they are primarily concerned with a detailed diagnosis. This initial diagnosis allows them, for example, to react properly to a patient's swallowing problem. The treatment could be different depending on whether the cause is a common, feverish cold or, perhaps, a laryngeal or throat cancer. The educational measures that we routinely rely on often correspond to the futile attempt to treat an emerging cancer with throat lozenges. Sometimes, however, we choose the opposite reaction: We prescribe a difficult operation to treat a slight cold.

TEN STEPS FOR JUSTIFYING A DISCIPLINARY ACTION

Table 6.1

Phase	Core questions
Diagnosis	What information do we have about the life, past experiences, and the potential of the child or teenager who is provoking us?
	How can we characterize the value of these behavioral activities?
	What is actually bothering the child or teenager?
Therapy	What "drugs" have already been tried without success?
	Has this ineffective medication truly been abandoned?
	Is there a "homeopathic" cure?
	What about the power of self-healing?
Rehabilitation	What do we prescribe as the posttreatment therapy?
	How do we organize the return to daily life?
	What outpatient care is required?

In this specific case, the new viewpoint of the teachers was just able to change gradually the behavior of the provocative student. Just the fact that they took the time for a thorough diagnosis of Johnny's disturbing behavior and no longer reacted to the symptoms opened a whole new perspective and with that came a new relationship for Johnny. He felt the change in climate and—although he never wanted to admit it—he felt better in the new friendlier environment. Although he continued his provocations as before, the teachers somehow found it easier to deal with them, no longer considered them so important, and let his escapades pass without comments, in order to simply carry on as before. In parallel, Johnny noticed that even when he did not call attention to himself through provocations, he would receive the same interest and openness from the teachers—an experience that was totally new and strange to him. Gradually, he grew to trust their openness and, even for himself, learned that he could turn to his teachers with his questions and problems.

Other tips for a diagnostics-based educational response are:

- Do not react to the symptoms, rather, react to the cause!
- Do not make your opinion of the child or teenager depending on his behavior alone!
- Remember: the more "extreme" the provocation of others, the more severe the diagnosis is likely to be!
- Base your actions on the principle: the more severe the diagnosis, the more intense the treatment and care must be!
- Completely discontinue once and for all, the use of "drugs" that have proven ineffective!

Textbox 6.3

The teaching staff noticed that after they had been practicing the new strategy "Search for the impressions behind the expression!" for some time, they very rarely complained about "difficult" students or their behavior. Rather, they had grown accustomed to looking at these students as customers and to focusing on them as individuals. In the process, they also noticed that the change in how they viewed these young people was what allowed everything else to change. Suddenly, the children experienced themselves differently, and they changed.

Surprise with an unexpected reaction!

Many disciplinary measures are doomed to fail from the start because, ultimately, they can be anticipated and calculated by the child or teenager. This signals the end of any educational effect because education "lives" by or through generating the willingness and the *will* to bring about change in another. We can be certain that the original educational goal we had hoped for has truly been achieved only when the child actually demonstrates the expected attitude or behavior. Behaviors achieved through threats are superficial and are effective only in the short term. This form of compliance is adaption, not education, that is, forced, not voluntary.

> *Education is not a "trade." It is not about a socially desired or even forced behavior. Children and teenagers can advance in their behavioral development only if they experience a resonance that can affect their behavior over the long term and lead to positive change.*

Teenagers who have skipped school for several days "expect" to be reprimanded, that extra work will be required of them (in the "detention hall"), or even that their parents will be invited to meet with the teacher because those are what past experiences have taught them. Of course, the offender must be aware of the possible consequences or punishments. However, are such expected reactions truly effective? Does sitting out a punishment actually increase the likelihood that the student will attend class more regularly in the future?

In the case of repeated delinquencies, avoid expected disciplinary reactions. Apply the general rule: If it is expected, it will soon fade. The long-term benefit of discipline is always a behavioral change as a result of vigorous experiences. Ask yourself the question: How can I use a surprising reaction to irritate, confront, and inspire the child or teenager?

UNEXPECTED REACTIONS

Textbox 7.1

At a secondary school, a teenager was absent from school for two months without an excuse and was not punished by the school or the teacher. In an interview, a teacher said, "Yes, well, what actually happened? The student did not attend class. He was in France during this time in order to help one of our exchange students in a family matter: certainly, this is not our official school curriculum; however, it was also not a typical truancy from which nothing is learned! This is the reason we decided, in this case, to react differently: the student was asked to clearly explain what skills he was able to develop over this two-month period and how these are to be assessed against the background of the failed material. First, he had to explain these skills in a credible way and then he had to present a plan as to how he would make up the 'failed' classes."

This form of disciplinary reaction is not only surprising; it also presumes that the other person is responsible. Such a response impressively demonstrates the three basic tenets in all forms of education: "The advancement of learning, the individual and the social conduct" (Bennack 2006, p. 69). The students are not merely reprimanded or punished, but, instead, given an opportunity to assess, in a responsible way, the consequences of their behavior for their own academic development, and even to find ways to overcome the shortcomings. In parallel, the students' feelings of self-responsibility are strengthened by the assumption that there are "good reasons" for the conduct and that they are capable of planning and self-directed learning. The "tenet" of social conduct is not only expressed by the fact that the absence from class served to help a friend, but also in the attitude, apparent to all and demonstrated by the teacher, that—even if we find it surprising, annoying, or shocking—people usually act out of "good reason," which, in principal, should always be assumed and respected. Finally, we trust that they are capable of being answerable for their own behavior—as in the given example, when the student took responsibility for justifying the behavior and planning the makeup classes into his own hands.

> Self-responsibility can develop only if students are truly "allowed" to accept the responsibility for their actions. In other words, change your perspective—the opinion you have formed of the student. Picture them not just as "rule-breakers," but rather as someone who may have "good reasons" for their behavior and who can plan a way to make up for the work missed, admit errors, and make amends! Surprise the child or teenager by not responding with punishment, but rather with encouragement and trust!

It is helpful to adopt a set of questions that can help you in specific disciplinary situations in order not to fall—again—into a judgmental role when responding to deviant behavior. What is important is that you convey a confidence-building and trust in the child.

THE QUESTIONS OF TRUST

The following table presents an overview of seven confidence-building questions:

Table 7.1

How does the child or teenager explain and "justify" his behavior to himself and to others?
What does the child or teenager think about the effects of such behavior on us or others? (Frequently asked question: What do you think your friends would think of what you are doing?)
What does the child or teenager consider to be an appropriate response by those around him (teachers, parents, etc.) to the behavior?
What does the child or teenager believe would makeup for the failures or repair the damage that has occurred?
How does the child or teenager want to take responsibility for restoring a suitable balance?
Does the child or teenager know what adverse effects the conduct has on his or her own development (e.g., academic failures)?
What suggestions does the child or teenager have?

These questions of trust serve as the doors to an educational dialog, as the educator-philosopher Martin Buber explained. In the educational dialog, "reciprocity" is the fundamental concept. Parents and teachers should always try to experience, "from the other side," what the child or teenager feels about their expectations. Specifically, this refers to more than the mere ability to empathize with the ideas of the child or adolescent in order to discover their motivations and logic. Actually, this refers to addressing the child or adolescent as a responsible person, assuming this person is capable of giving reasons for the behavior and of assessing the consequences.

In this dialog, the teacher does not only refer to the child or teenager, but rather lets them participate in the world of responsibility. Of course, this applies not only when we determine a deviation and disturbance of the rules. Rather, this participation should always resonate in the way we deal with the child or adolescent—even in situations where we are not aware of discipline.

Education is not only occasional; rather, it is an expression and a result of a continuous dialog.

Martin Buber:

I point to the child lying there, with half-closed eyes, awaiting the words of the mother. But some children do not have to wait: they already know. They are constantly addressed in a never ending conversation. Faced with the threat of a lonely night, they lie there sheltered and protected, invulnerable in the silver, chain armor of trust. Confident and trusting in the world, because of such people—that is the inner most aim of the parenting relationship. Because of such people, the absurdity cannot be the reality, no matter how hard it is threatening. (1986, p. 40)

Respond with levelheadedness and always be consequential!

"Stay consequential? That is difficult enough, but a levelheaded response? That is easier said than done when my students are climbing over the desks." These are the words frequently heard as the response from overburdened parents or stressed teachers. Many times the urgent effort to first restore order is of such priority that the sensible part gets left behind. For those with educational responsibilities, the question is: How do I handle a disciplinary situation in which I feel so overwhelmed that I cannot apply my good sense?

Textbox 8.1

A young mother came to the parenting counseling session fully exhausted and completely burned out: "I simply cannot take my children any longer. As soon as I get the one to sit down and do homework, the two little ones are at loggerheads and breaking each other's toys. And while I turn to make peace there, the older one starts surfing the Internet again even though I have forbidden it. I need to split myself into two or even into three. What really nerves me most: the noise and the constant fussing at home drives me to the point that I just want to run away screaming! Day after day, it's the same thing and I often dread the afternoons."

SURVEY THE SITUATION AND STAY CALM

Those responsible for educating—those who see themselves confronted with similar overwhelming situations—often have lost sight of the big picture. They feel their energy being drained by failures and are unable to get out of the hamster wheel of unsuccessful efforts. It would be unusual to find a single great piece of advice that could free them from their dilemma. What is needed is a variety of potentially successful measures, which they can select from to build an effective teaching environment.

Only those who can reflect can act wisely. The success of your disciplinary response depends on your knowing not only what you want, but also what is possible. If you rely only on your spontaneous reactions, you risk losing any hope of success. If you know what is essential, you must then skillfully dispense the measures that will end the discordance.

Specific disciplinary problems always demand the use of good DISCORD resolution skills on the part of those responsible. Although, there is never a guarantee of success for your disciplinary actions when dealing with children and your actions are subject to a "no refunds" policy, you can still check to see whether you have actually thought about the seven aspects of sensible and consequential parenting. Disciplinary situations are always new and different. Consequently, parents and educators need to have a differentiated view, which helps them see clearly what has to be done and what is better left alone.

Skillfully dispensing the disciplinary measures to prevent discord implies that you understand your own expectations and are clear about what you are prepared to do to ensure the child's or teenager's behavior reflects these expectations.

A major part of being in a position of responsibility is learning to balance your own expectations and disciplinary measures, and not reacting spontaneously if you find yourself unable to cope with a situation. Such spontaneous reactions are often out of proportion and inappropriate in a given situation and are poorly understood by the other person and are seldom taken seriously.

Effective discipline requires the child to take seriously what we say and do. Although we cannot force them to do this, we can help them by presenting a clear, predictable, and consistent front. In this way, we become a visible, known quantity in the child's realm of experience and will no longer be perceived as sometimes blowing hot and cold.

SEVEN ASPECTS OF PREVENTING DISCORD

Textbox 8.2

Declaration
You must clearly tell (announce) your children or students the five types of behavior you are not prepared to accept. They must know what consequences they will face when they violate your expectations. Define a catalog of fines and discuss it with your children!

Initiative
You must define the framework. Take the time to describe very precisely what you expect, what violations you take very seriously, and what you are prepared to do to enforce the defined framework.

Self-protection
Protect yourself from excessive demands and aggression. Rethink if you are really always in demand! Find a room where you can physically escape, where you will not always be at the center of events. Delegate responsibility (to older children, the class speaker, or someone else responsible).

Composure
Never determine these provisions when you are upset. Keep a clear head when thinking about your concept of discipline. Think about the happiness you receive from your children and try and imagine how they may test your framework ("the five unacceptable forms of behavior") and catalog of fines.

Organization
Define exactly when you will verify compliance with the rules (for example, "a clean room") and how you will react at the moment of a violation (for example, "aggression"). Establish a specific place where you can announce your decisions.

(cont...)

Textbox 8.2 *(cont...)*

Relief

Look for opportunities when you can relax. You do not have to watch your children constantly. Ask yourself what are the times that your children could be with a babysitter or at the day-care center or with someone else (for example, uncles, aunts, and friends). Change provides you with the chance to experience other things and also to be different.

Determination

If you have defined a consequence, then always be sure to enforce it. Most disciplinary problems arise through inconsistency when you blow both hot and cold. This is ineffective and overwhelms the child (they are not sure of what is happening).

Create emotions if they have grown cold!

This rule comes from Haim Omer (University of Tel Aviv) and Arist von Schlippe (University Witten-Herdecke). Both authors give the parents of children "with behavioral problems" (Omer/von Schlippe 2006) an unusual piece of advice. They suggest the use of some kind of nonviolent resistance against the child's conduct when nothing else seems to work. In place of ineffective arguments, appeals, and threats, "when words no longer have any effect" try to use nonviolent methods (Omer/von Schlippe 2005, p. 41). The two behavioral scientists write:

> The paradoxical phenomenon that verbal arguments, pleadings and explanations have the opposite effect as intended is well-known to the parents of aggressive children. The more they talk, the more the child is convinced that parents are not prepared to act. Parental talks serve as a guaranty that the child can do what it wants. For this reason, many children, especially adolescents, try to involve their parents in debates. They know from experience that their parents will not act as long as they are talking. Parental talks can also be damaging if they provide the energy for escalation: The parent's request turns to a demand and the demand turns into a threat. The child pays back in the same coinage: Arguments are answered with louder arguments and threats with more severe counter-threats. Sometimes, the escalation frightens the parents so much that they return to their soft pleading—a swing of the pendulum that, nevertheless, also contributes to escalation: The child responds to the softening position of the parents with contempt and stronger demands. The negative cycle can be interrupted when parents learn how to avoid being drawn into escalating verbalizations: "Strike the iron when it is cold!" (ibid., pp. 41 and 43)

This saying can be interpreted as a principle of systemic and effective parenting:

> Avoid the "trap of escalation" in the argumentative education strategy. If you do not accept your child's behavior, you must signal loud and clear: "I am not going to accept this situation any longer and will do everything in my power to stop it, except for physical or verbal abuse." (see ibid., p. 231)

If parents succeed in turning to nonviolence—even verbally—they can free themselves from their passive and often merely reactionary role and can win back their position and play an active role. At the same time, they extract themselves from the never-ending debates, which, for quite some time, have stressed or even begun to destroy any relationship with their children. The essential message to the child is: "I am in control here and I take my responsibility seriously!"

FORMS AND PRINCIPLES OF NONVIOLENT RESISTANCE

The main forms and principles of nonviolent resistance for parents to use against the behavior of their child are listed in table 9.1.

Haim Omer and Arist von Schlippe reported the case of Amelie, who retreated more and more "into her cave" and wouldn't come out, as well as her strange eating habits, and compulsive behavior throughout the day. Her parents were overwhelmed and decided to seek out a family therapist:

> *The therapist recommended that the parents enter Amelie's room together and remain there for three hours. The mother could tidy up the room (Amelie had long since abandoned any sense of order, her room was a mess). If Amelie became violent, the father should prevent them from coming to blows. The therapist would keep the line open round the clock for telephone calls. The aim was to challenge Amelie's unquestioned territorial unassailability and bring her to the negotiating table.*
>
> *The reaction was incredibly swift. The father's scratched cheek, the mother's black eye were the only casualties from the altercation. As the father tried to hold her back, Amelie began to scream. She screamed for*

Table 9.1

Forms and principles of nonviolence	Experiences
(1) Step out of the vicious circle: resist the provocations (refuse to be drawn in), practice the principle of delayed response.	Enables a respectful role for the parents or a role that regains respect (since the
(2) Announce the use of the language of "objective facts."	other still has nonviolent interests).
(3) Sit-in: a reaction immediately after an altercation, deliberately wait for the child to suggest an alternative.	Demonstrates the ineffectiveness of the other's violent conduct
(4) Break the code of silence: appoint supporters and agents, go public, name the deeds (e.g., violence and coercion), write letters to friends and relatives.	which, sooner or later, will cease.
(5) The telephone list: call friends and their parents (e.g., if the child does not come home at night).	
(6) Follow-up and research.	. . . Show the child that
(7) The prolonged strike: a 3-day sit-in (for serious, i.e., criminal acts) with the participation of many friends and relatives.	you are outside of the systemic dynamic, that you will act
(8) Insubordination: end the service, break the taboos (e.g., go to the school).	autonomously and with dignity (e.g., services
(9) Gestures of reconciliation: for example, recognition, common undertakings (not as a reward).	denied), and that you trust the other to find a proper solution.

over an hour. Then she started to whimper and kept that up for another two hours of the sit-in. Towards the end of the third sit-in hour, Amelie began to talk. Initially she sought out a coalition with the father against the mother. Failing that, she decided to negotiate. No further sit-ins were necessary. Amelie ate meals again with the family. After several weeks, she went shopping with her mother (something she had not done since she was fifteen). She returned to her part-time job and decided to attend the university. She has kept up her grades for the last two years and has never again locked herself in her room. (Omer/von Schlippe 2006, p. 96f).

Such experience illustrates that parents do not have to surrender, but, rather, they can change the situation through an active presence (I am in charge). The fundamental step is the one to a different disciplinary attitude, where it is no longer necessary to be right or even to have the last word. The important thing is for parents to become active and reclaim their dignity and step off the never-ending ladder of verbal confrontation and escalation. They demonstrate, in a determined and courageous way, what it is they expect and are prepared to enforce. In his "Principles of nonviolent resistance—instructions for parents," Haim Omer gives parents the following advice:[1]

Textbox 9.1

"Parents, who frequently allow themselves to be drawn into altercations with their children tend to talk a lot, to preach, to debate, to excuse, to justify, to scream, to convince and to reciprocate . . . :

Note:

- Each of these reactions signals being drawn into a fight.
- Each form of being drawn in leads to escalation!
  . . .
- Too much talk is an escalation.
- Too much talking is a sign of helplessness.
- Clear statements lead to fewer escalations as the attempts to convince, to preach, and to debate.
  . . .
- Setting conditions on an overbearing child in order to force a desired behavior carries the risk of sharpening the escalation. The child always responds with new terms and conditions.
- With such children, it is always better to avoid conditions (if . . . then).
  . . .
- Write your reactions down! Take the time to plan your reaction!
- If in doubt, remain silent and do not respond. Silence is not surrender!"

NOTE

1. www.suchthilfe.biz/Elternanleitung.pdf.

Direct your parenting measures at the behavior, not at the person!

This parenting rule may sound obvious—but it is not. When children or teenagers challenge, overwhelm, or even make thoughtless comments that are perceived by adults as rude and insulting, they often react just as thoughtlessly. Not infrequently, one word leads to another and there are cases where parents find themselves terribly insulted. Educational counselors sometimes even report cases in which, for example, a teenage son tells his mother "where she can go" when borrowing the car—often accompanied by more disrespectful behavior.

Textbox 10.1

> One mother broke into tears as she related how her son repeatedly called her a "stupid fool" and finally bellowed out: "I'm not letting you tell me anything! You can't even get your own life under control and you want to tell me what to do." She was completely desperate and said, "I am still responsible for him. What will become of him now?"

In such a situation it is important to be very clear about what is actually going on and what can be expected. Of course, the mother is concerned that her son appears so arrogant and is so offensive even at his vocational school and workplace. However, it is important that this mother first makes it clear that it comes down to the question of what harm results from the behavior of her son. A lack of respect is only tolerated by those who are unsure of themselves in the parenting role or, perhaps, even in the role of an adult. A true credo says:

Only those who respect themselves can command respect.

OFFER THE CHILD AN ABLE ADVERSARY

This is an area where things are often in a sorry state. When children hold the trump card, parents have mostly given up, or they experience themselves as ineffective—and not just in educational issues. Parents are often anxious to maintain harmony in their relationship with their child or teenager at nearly any cost. They think arguments and conflicts are harmful, and they don't realize that by repeatedly giving in, they are gradually undermining their own authority. Children seek confrontation with an opponent and the question is whether parents are really willing and able to present themselves as this adversary and, instead of avoiding the conflicts, actually deal with them.

Are you a good adversary for your child?	Often	Rarely	Never
I listen to descriptions, reports, and worries, without expressing my own thoughts and opinions right away.			
I state my expectations in a clear and friendly tone and also define the consequences of breaking the rules.			
If the rules are violated, I don't react emotionally, rather objectively and consistently.			
I use the same tone of friendly and open speech—even if I was disappointed or am punishing some misbehavior			
In principle, I trust my children to solve the problems and conflicts they face.			

Figure 10.1

According to Jesper Juul, a Danish educational counselor:

Most children—whether at home, in kindergarten, or in school—are able to resolve their conflicts on their own; not actually needing the supervision of adults. The idea that adults can resolve all conflict in a sensible way is nice, but not realistic. As an adult, you can hope that your children will be able to express their problems when they are 20-year olds; that may be a praiseworthy educational aim for your efforts. But, it is simply impossible to expect that from a five or six-year old.

One more important thought: All conflicts, that have meaning in life, are produced from an aggressive tone. Our annoyances, our frustration, our anger needs to be first expressed in order for us to transform it—we need these emotions, just as we need happiness and satisfaction to deal with the reality. (Juul 2005, p. 129)

CREATE A CULTURE OF HEALTHY CONFLICT

Effective education "lives," namely, from the adult culture of conflict. A culture of conflict refers to our ability to go a reasonable distance to meet the other and to clearly define our limits as well as the consequences ("I simply cannot accept this!") and, at the same time, to maintain the relationship ("You are still my child!"). This implies three things:

- Conflicts are not scandals; rather they add the salt of life to every real human relationship. We cooperate by arguing things out and tolerating opposites, different opinions and interests, and by learning to constructively assert ourselves in conflict situations.
- Conflicts are not solved by emotional outbursts and helplessly screaming your view out into the void, or by reaching for draconian measures; rather, they are solved only by clearly stating your expectations and what your reaction will be if the behavior you find disruptive repeats itself.
- Conflicts are not solved by responding, for example, to an insult with another insult and in the process contributing to the escalation of the communication. Solutions require rather a clear differentiation between the behavior expressed and the person expressing it.

In summary, when your children insult you or when students disrespect their teachers, those responsible for discipline are faced with the difficult job of finding an appropriate response, yet, at the same time, not ruining the relationship. The problem that often overwhelms parents or teachers is this: we love our children and care about our students, but we cannot accept their conduct. We must always separate the two—the love, on one hand, and the disapproval, on the other—a difficult thing to balance, indeed.

The basic parenting advice in this context is: be clear and consistent in your if-then declarations ("If this behavior happens again, I will . . ."), but never resentful. Education works through firm consequences, not by withholding love and affection!

Childhood and teenage development requires both: a relationship and unconditional love on the one hand, and a serious opponent on the other. This opposition must come across as factual, friendly, and not inconsequential. Adolescents see the adult world in this adversary, which is a world with consequences. Again and again, however, we blur the boundaries of these two areas with our care and love just as our desire for harmony takes over exactly at that moment when we should be consequential.

If our children learn that we do not truly mean the things we say, we deprive them of the important opportunity of experiencing the consequences of their own actions. Yet, experiencing the consequences is just the thing that forms character and personal responsibility. If a child or teenager experiences the consequences of one's actions, they gain insight and maturity, and the willingness to try other forms of behavior.

Many disciplinary problems stem from this mixture of love and inconsequential responses. Frequently, it even comes to a reversal of the relationship ("I big, you small"). At that point, good advice is expensive. Before you can finally put an end to such behavior, it is necessary to exercise your own power as an adult and clearly express the conduct that will no longer be tolerated.

Practice consistency in child rearing!

Many self-help guides to parenting note two serious drawbacks when sanctions are inconsistently enforced: First, they are ineffective over the middle and long term; second, children and adolescents learn fairly quickly that the policies of those responsible for education—luckily—are inconsequential. Inconsistent enforcement weakens the very core of the relationship, that is, the predictability and clarity of the adult world, in contrast to the searching of the adolescent.

Rules without consequences are like swimming without water! But remember, consequences without rules serve only your emotional venting, not the insight of the adolescent!

For this reason, "consistency training" for parents and educators is of fundamental importance. Consequential discipline must be practiced and learned. Before making every disciplinary response, you must be clear as to what effect will result from your intended response. Some details are provided below in the "Ten commands of consequential parenting."

Textbox 11.1

The ten commands of consequential parenting

Command #1
Parenting is not a part-time job. It requires your attention and care. Always think about whether you are willing and able to effectively enforce the announced consequence.

(cont...)

Textbox 11.1 *(cont...)*

Command #2

Take full advantage of an opportunity (e.g., when faced with an incident) to explain to your children or students the rules of the game. Construct your if-then clauses!

Command #3

You can discuss, transform, and "agree" on your educational principles and even formulate joint "rules of togetherness" in your classroom. However, do not do this during an actual conflict situation.

Command #4

Write your educational rules or "rules of togetherness" down and make sure your children also take note of them. The transparency of valid rules is the most important prerequisite for their effectiveness.

Command #5

Always ensure that the enforcement of your rules is perceived as a consequence of their own behavior and not meant to insult or humiliate.

Command #6

Ensure that there are no exceptions to the rules and that these will be applied—irrespective of the person.

Command #7

The consequence is a measure initiated by the one responsible for educating. For a consequential lesson, ensure that when formulating the rules, the consequences you announce are the ones you can actually implement.

Command #8

If an educational consequence must be applied, consider your personal relationship with the offender.

(cont...)

Textbox 11.1 *(cont...)*

Command #9
Never be vindictive. The actual consequence should also be a chance for the child or teenager to make amends for the harm.

Command #10
Remember your own pranks, bickering, and intransigence and always recognize yourself in the child or teenager.

Being consequent is not the same as moralizing. Rules must be discussed with the child or teenager *before* the problems arise; the child must know what to expect. No policy in child rearing can be retroactive: no punishment can be imposed for the infringement of a "law" that was unknown at the time of the violation. Rules cannot be "announced" spontaneously and perhaps even as an expression of great anger. Children do not learn from your annoyance, but, rather, from their own sobering if-then experiences and from knowing that they can make amends for the harm they have done.

Textbox 11.2

A 12-year-old girl left home one evening through the window of her room in order to meet with her friends. When the parents went to check on her and found the empty bed, they broke out with inconsolable excitement. After a long and unsuccessful search, they alerted the police, who with several officers conducted a search of the immediate vicinity and finally turned to the friends' parents. After a long search, they discovered three girls in a nearby abandoned factory where they had made a small campfire and were telling each other ghost stories. Of course, the parents were greatly relieved to be able to hug their daughter again, but they also knew that it was time for a "consequential" response.

Their daughter had broken the rule about not going out after dark without her parents. Just recently, the parents had discussed the case

(cont...)

Textbox 11.2 *(cont...)*

of a small child in northern Germany who had disappeared and had been found dead several days later in Belgium. They had also told her about the consequences she would face if she broke this rule. "You have to know," said the father, "that there are boundaries that you cannot cross without having to pay the consequences. This is especially true for situations when you do not do what we expect in the interests of your own safety. You have to know that we worry about you if you do not come home on time or if it is suddenly dark outside and you are still out in the street. If this ever happens again, you will get a week of house arrest and if that is not enough, we will take away your computer for a while! So you better think twice if you ever get the urge to sneak out again!"

Certainly, the announced sanction may be too drastic in some cases and there may be differences of opinion on that, however, the important point is that the child or teenager knows in advance what the consequences will be for that behavior.

In effective parenting, the consequences may never catch the child or teenager off guard. A child does not learn from being at a disadvantage which gives the feeling of being exposed, but rather from the experience that he can rely on the parents and their rules. This is why the opposite is also true: Avoid consequences that have not been announced! Consequences without rules are arbitrary and, sadly, can only be observed, but never understood.

Exercise your "parental presence" — the key to effective parenting!

Only parents, and those responsible for education, can determine their own behavior, not the behavior of their children. For all the problems with which they find themselves confronted, it always comes down to the sole issue: "How can I conduct myself in a way that clearly shows the other person how I am feeling?" Parents or teachers cannot influence whether and to what extent the child or adolescent feels addressed or even chastened by their reactions.

The only thing educators can do is to ask: Am I sending a message that opens the "effectiveness channels" or the one that shuts them down?

What are the "effectiveness channels" that an adult can open to children and adolescents? This is another question that cannot be answered by simple assumptions! This is because education works indirectly and rarely is it immediate. The willingness to behave in one way or another is totally up to the child. Whether or not one is aware of it, what helps the child to decide is the permanent presence of what is unconditionally given, that is, parental love, or—at school—the professional care and attention of the teacher. The Israeli educational scientist Haim Omer and his German colleague Arist von Schlippe use the term "parental presence" for both situations and suggest it as the key to effective parenting:

Parental presence is not a standard concept. If yielding to the child becomes the rule, the child is denied the parental presence. And even worse, at some level, the child feels it has eliminated the presence of the parents. (. . .) Having a presence means being someone, someone with their own thoughts, feelings, and desires. In order to develop, a child needs someone like that. Only such a figure, that has a personal presence, is able to give a child the feeling of security and acceptance. (Omer and von Schlippe 2006, p. 30)

PARENTAL PRESENCE THROUGH THOUGHTFULNESS

Parental presence has nothing to do with the physical presence of the parent or the teacher. They may be physically present, yet still not really present. The opposite may also be the case: even in families where the parents no longer live together, they may both be educationally present for the child. Therefore, the question is, how is parental presence expressed? It is the moment of thoughtfulness, which, to define simply, means: the attitude with which I meet my child—lovingly and with an open interest—while at the same time, demonstrating what a responsible life means. For this reason, I never shackle or bully my child, but I am also not prepared for unlimited flexibility. Parental (or educational) presence is unthinkable without thoughtfulness, which is why parents, and those responsible for education, are well advised to first consider whether and to what extent they are capable of thoughtful dealings with the child or the adolescent entrusted to their care. The checklist in figure 12.1 may help you.

If you have quietly completed this checklist in all sincerity to yourself, you can now use the "never" or "rarely" answers to help you search for the opportunities that may help you improve, in the future, on these aspects of your parental presence. Perhaps you also found additional encouragement by the statement that the ability for parental presence—according to everything educational research tells us—is the true guaranty for effectiveness in all education. When children and teenagers experience "parents they can rely on," they develop a strong reserve of trust, which they can fall back on even in difficult situations, cases of misconduct, or academic failures.

Often, parenting problems arise when this "presence" is not (no longer) practiced by the parents and is not experienced by the children. Children or adolescents start to look for resonance somewhere else in order to explore their limits and challenge the adults.

11 Aspects of Parental Presence	I can	Never	Rarely	Often
Good listener	... be approached at any time by my children if they have a concern or a problem.			
Coach	... listen to my children and support them in finding solutions, without proposing my own solutions in haste.			
Heart bonder	... love my children—no matter what they do and what may become of them—and give them the feeling they are a part of me.			
Tolerance	... stand it when my children are sometimes difficult and behave foolishly; I clearly mark the boundaries and I am not usually resentful.			
Worry box	... feel it when something is bothering my children, and more and more they share it with me on their own.			
Attorney	... stand up for my children—especially if they have made mistakes and caused trouble for others.			
Mediator	... listen to different points of view and arbitrate the conflict so the participants can come to an agreement.			
Consequential	... abide by agreements and, when there are consequences to be paid, I do not negotiate.			
Cheerleader	... encourage my children over and over again to try on their own to solve a problem and explicitly praise successful efforts.			
Interested	... always show interest in each of my children and have conversations in which they can present their interests and concerns in detail.			
Loyal	... vouch for my children, i.e., there is no conduct that could make me permanently turn my back on my child.			

Figure 12.1

Many educational problems can be more appropriately understood as a search for resonance than simply interpreted as a delinquent behavior and tracked in the parental punishment log or school records. Practicing parental presence in the family, where it can be lived and experienced, represents an important prophylaxis against the emergence of an educational impasse.

Your own educational responsibility does not start when you are confronted by the problematic behavior of your child or student. It begins at the moment a child or student is entrusted into your care. That is when you must ask yourself, "How good is my ability to form a parental presence?" You may need to make a greater effort to be even more present!

The topic of "parental presence" shows that to deal successfully with disciplinary problems, parents and educators need more than just a few quick tips and tricks or some pithy slogans like "In Praise of Education" (Bueb 2007) or "Teenage Tyrants" (Weikert 1994). The self-help parenting guides that advertise with promises to deliver "Survival Strategies for Troubled Parents" are not only unreliable; but also, rather, harmful. Such views are still based on the basic message of finger pointing "You are not OK." Such messages are catchy and flattering—but unfortunately, ineffective! Their popularity is based on the fact that stressed parents and teachers are not obliged to take responsibility on themselves.

Only if you investigate your problem, and determine the extent to which it is exacerbated or maybe even caused by the fact your parental presence has long been skewed, can you take hold of the tiller and return to course and establish once again your presence.

Put your parenting practices under the "macroscope" and discover what is preventing your children from doing their homework!

A daily annoyance for teachers: students who once again have not done their homework. Nearly every teacher is aware of the ineffectiveness of warnings, extra work, and poor grades. Usually, such measures only accelerate the process of exclusion and academic failure—a process that could perhaps be stopped if they only knew how. Parents are often powerless when a note is sent home from school and the teacher is requesting a meeting. The domestic storm, which rages down on their children as a result, also does not have the effect that the teacher hoped it would have. The children promise to change in the future, but renewed complaints soon follow.

Textbox 13.1

The eighth-grade teacher was at his wit's end. It seems Kevin, who is really "a well-mannered" student—as another teacher characterized him—is drawing more and more attention to himself by not doing his assigned homework. He always turns on his charm to explain to the teacher he simply could not find the time. Finally, the teacher decided to write a note to his parents stating: "Please ensure that your son Kevin's deviant behavior in the classroom regarding the completion of his school assignments does not occur in the future!" After a few days had passed, the teacher received a note from the parents that made him think. It said, "Please ensure that your student Kevin's deviant behavior at home regarding his domestic chores does not occur in the future!"

This exchange of correspondence shows all too clearly that educational measures are frequently of the pleading kind: A grievance is aired and a third party is sought out—the parents or the principal or the best friend—who, it is thought, is the one who can "talk some sense" into the delinquent child—a futile action, which, all involved, can actually see after the third or fourth time. What can be done?

TRADE IN THE PARENTING MICROSCOPE FOR A PARENTING MACROSCOPE!

A microscope is used to see things in their smallest parts as accurately as possible. In an educational context, the general belief is that you can solve a problem by analyzing it in detail, looking very carefully at the individual components. Sometimes this ends up sending children with behavioral problems to psychological or even medical examinations, which end with a cocktail of therapeutic measures or, frequently, a cocktail of drugs (see Rule 14). The child becomes a case, and their environment degenerates into a *problem trance*, that is, a state in which they are perceived through the lens of deviant behavior. So quickly, we make a mountain out of a molehill, and instead of an academic career, a career of prescribed measures has begun.

The view through the educational macroscope is different: the focus is not on the detail (in this example, the repeated failure to do homework), but, rather, on the behavior as it relates to a larger picture. This coarser macroscopic focus lets the child come into focus in a context where the overall behavior is the subject. As far as the failure to do the assigned homework is concered, there is a difference between the student who is at risk of graduating and the student who is actually performing quite well in the school. The key macroscopic questions are:

> What is "my" child or student trying to express by not doing the homework? What does the homework really have to do with learning success? How important is it to me?

The view through the educational macroscope can lead us to the additional questions that we would never have come to consider if we took the microscopic view of the problem of the child's refusing to do homework.

THESE "MACROSCOPIC" QUESTIONS ARE:

Table 13.1

Focus	Macroscopic question	Follow-up question
Performance	How does the child or adolescent perform in other areas? What motivates them to perform when required?	(1) What do I know about the performance in other areas? (2) Do I know the issues and areas in which the child or adolescent may develop strong talents?
Reliability	When does the child or adolescent act reliably and when unreliably?	(3) In what areas can I rely 100 percent on the trustworthiness of the child or adolescent? (4) Do I explicitly appreciate this reliability? Or has it been overshadowed by the cases of unreliability?
Distractions	What might be distracting (e.g., hobby, PC, home environment) the child or adolescent?	(5) What do I actually know about the daily life of the child or adolescent? (6) Am I supportive in questions of how to manage many things at one time?
Understanding	Is the assignment too difficult or too easy for the child or adolescent?	(7) Is there a lack of knowledge, skill, or talent to complete the tasks? (8) Have I provided ample opportunity to practice independent work and learning?
Point	What is the point of the assignment? Is my homework pointless for the child or adolescent?	(9) What is the point of the homework in terms of the child's or the adolescent's practicing and learning? (10) What can I do to make the homework meaningful to the child or adolescent?

When parents and teachers learn to operate the educational macroscope, they expand their range of options for dealing with the problem. Simultaneously, they avoid looking through an extremely focused lens and seeing deviant behavior in their child's statement ("I don't do homework!"). A macroscopic view does not imply that homework is no longer important. Rather, it is more about looking for alternatives that will make doing the homework more likely to happen. Using a macroscope, parents and teachers will ask what roles do performance, reliability, distraction, understanding, and meaning have in the life of "their" children. Those who can step back and look at the overall situation may realize that there are areas in the child's life where it is certainly alright to rely on the child and they will see that the child is able to commit and achieve things. Consequently, such a macroscopic focus alone may free the frustrated teacher or angry father from the *problem trance*.

If your child does not do the homework, look at it through an educational macroscope. Take advantage of the opportunity you have to recognize the potentials and build on these. You may, for example, assign a familiar topic or a topic of interest to the child so they would like to develop it further.

Teachers and those responsible for educating must determine their own approach and not that of the child or adolescent. For this reason, in terms of the homework you assign, specifically ask yourself if the topic is really a suitable one.

In the context of homework, limit yourself to the exercise of reinforcing what is actually covered, explained, and discussed in the classroom. Do not assign homework if you are not certain that it can be mastered by all students on their own.

Control your child's exposure time to television and other media!

Innovations have always been met with skepticism and suspicion. At the end of the nineteenth century, warnings and fears about the availability of books and novels prompted men to believe that women would neglect their "real chores" because of too much reading. The introduction of the first automobiles was accompanied by the fear of high speeds, citing the belief that it is bad for your health. Similar fears and anxieties were widespread at the discovery of the radio, television, and Internet. Many parents today cannot understand what their children do as they sit for hours in front of the PC and participate less and less in family activities or in spending time with their friends.

Textbox 14.1

A technically gifted father told me about an agreement he made with his 12-year-old son not to spend more than two hours per day on his PC. However, he often lost track of the time while surfing the Internet, so the father programmed an alarm clock through which the PC would shut down after two hours automatically—an example of a technical solution to an ongoing issue that strongly dominates many parent-child relationships in our society. Over time, however, the father began to wonder why the two hours of computer time seemed to last for such a long time. He then examined the computer and found that his son was also technically gifted. He had figured a way to reset the computer clock and even how to turn it on and off!

We note: You cannot prohibit the influence of PC & Co. It is far better to try to talk and exchange ideas with the children and adolescents about their world, which may seem strange and incomprehensible in many ways to us. If you have children or are responsible for children you cannot confine yourself to your own world, you must, rather, be open to the world of the child and maybe even let them introduce you to their world.

> Join your child for a day out in cyberspace. Let them explain to you how this world functions and what interests them most. This even applies to watching television with them: Don't just watch the shows you like, but also watch children's programming with your kids.

Unfortunately, this path is already closed to many parents. The children already know what their parents think about the TV marathon, the "surfing," or the video nights (motto: "pizza, beer, and five videos"). They are suspicious of the parents' sudden interest in their preferences. When making the attempt to accompany your children, you must first try to get an invitation. The possible "door openers" include:

- Sit down when your children are watching a film and observe quietly what fascinates, interests, or amuses them!
- Gently ask questions and let them explain (e.g., who the characters are in a series you do not normally watch)!
- Communicate with your children in their social media (e.g., Facebook) and have someone help you while using a new computer.

Certainly: Some parents may react skeptically or even indignantly at such suggestions—"How am I supposed to open the door to their world?" These parents should be answered: "No, that is not the case! Of course, it is necessary to establish rules (for example, "No violent videos are allowed!") and viewing times!" But these rules are effective only if the children or adolescents feel their interests are not viewed through the lens of prohibitions or regulations. Young people also want to be treated with respect—even if what they do is, in your eyes, extremely "quirky" or problematic. This understanding can develop only if you allow yourself to keep the world of your children in mind. Our predispositions arise from what we are used to and what we think is right. Yet, how can we truly evaluate something if we do not know what it is?

> During these excursions into the media world of your children, avoid all the judgments and comments that could hurt the feelings of your child. Respect the fact that they have invited you. Take advantage of the opportunity to observe how your children deal with the broadcasts, programs, or computer games.

There are also voices that tell us that media is not only laden with doom for our children and teenagers. In this context, much attention was given to David Pfeiffer's book "How modern media makes us smarter" (Pfeiffer 2007). In this book, Pfeiffer argues that the new media also trains their minds and expands their horizons. In the following clear words, he brings educational research to the point:

> Television or video games do not make children stupid. But parents, who neglect the minds of their children, will most likely have no qualms about leaving their child all day in front of the TV. And, they are not shocked when their kids play shooting games for hours. The lack of discussion and the disinterest in such families are the problem—not the computers. It is a symptom of the neglect, not the cause. (ibid., p. 163)

This explains why prohibitive laws, such as the ones that the politicians always have ready at hand, actually achieve very little. In principle, we can and must ban the availability of the so-called killer games on the German markets to protect our children from questionable violent role models. Nevertheless, to believe this is an effective way to fight social neglect is to be sadly mistaken.

> You can only establish boundaries if you are familiar with the media world of your child and, for example, talk about why you do not want them to watch violent or sex videos.

RULES FOR THE MEDIA WORLD OF CHILDREN

In establishing effective boundaries, it makes little sense to merely designate forbidden rooms, because children and teenagers experience the media world and are confronted with its "temptations" not only at home, but also with friends, over mobile phones, or in school. The following rules may be of assistance:

Table 14.1

1. Ask yourself if you are talking enough with your kids or students about their questions, concerns, ideas, and interests! Expand the opportunities for togetherness and do not turn the spaces in which your children move into forbidden rooms!
2. Accompany your kids in their spaces without poisoning it by expressing your familiar skepticism, your commentary, or your accusations! Take advantage of the good fortune of being invited in and observe!
3. Wait until the third step to mark the boundaries and "forbidden" zones. Explain to the child why you do not want them to use certain offers (e.g., killer games). Ask yourself if you are willing and able to control this. Trust your children and make sure that you do not get yourself completely banished from their media world.
4. Be open to conversations about the questions, ambiguities, and contradictions that bother your children in relation to what they encounter in the media—take this seriously, even if you have no connection to these issues!
5. Pay attention to the skills they develop using the new media and promote this! Let them accompany you as you use the media yourself and let them experience how you choose among the offers, how you use your time, and how you reject other existing options.
6. Give your children the feeling that "something is happening" in everyday life outside the world of media and experience, discuss and enjoy things together.

Don't get forced into buying something just to avoid embarrassment!

Many parents are familiar with the supermarket problem: Given the huge selection of candies or other favorite sweets, some kids go crazy: "Daddy! I want those!" If refused ("You should not eat so much candy!") the child may start to cry or even throw a real tantrum. Many parents give in and "for the sake of peace" buy the child what she wants. Gabriele Kreter, in her parental advice book, suggests another solution. She recommends that parents in this situation follow the procedure shown below:

1. Keep a shopping list. Let the child participate by checking if there is enough milk, eggs, etc., in the refrigerator and corn flakes in the cabinet.
2. Show your child your wallet. "That is how much money we have. We have to spend it on what's on the list. I have no more money and we don't need anything else today."
3. Before you enter the supermarket, remind your child of the agreement. "You help me now to buy just the things on the list. If you whine, I will not help you!" (Kreter 2001, p. 99)

Kreter reports that after a few times, many children have learned to handle the temptations of the supermarket situation. If we examine the individual elements of this educational reaction, we can determine the following:

The situation is reinterpreted: From a huge selection of possibilities, a decision situation is presented, in which the child learns to buy only the necessities with the resources available.

This mechanism refers to a technique that can be applied in dealing with other educational problems: "Reframing" the situation, that is, giving it a different interpretation, can provide a range of different options. For example, a buying choice becomes a decision-making situation; accompaniment becomes participatory, fighting turns to a tempered response, or a "problem" becomes a challenge—to mention a few specific examples.

REFRAMING NEEDS TO BE PRACTICED

There are several questions that can help parents and educators to reframe (reinterpret) familiar educational problems:

Textbox 15.1

- What does the situation feel like to the other person (child, adolescent, class)?
- In what role do I place the other person because of how I arrange the situation (e.g., supermarket shopping trip)?
- What do I call the situation from the other person's point of view?
- How could I rename it?
- How would that change the roles and behavioral options of the other person?

Textbox 15.2

A father told me his experience with reframing his supermarket situation: His 8-year-old son quickly learned to check the refrigerator and take stock of what was there. He conducted a sort of interview with the father about what meals they wanted to prepare for the week in order to determine what needed to be bought. Then, he pretty much took charge of the shopping by picking the goods from the supermarket shelves, comparing prices, and making a kind of sport of discovering cheaper products. This was because he knew they had 100 dollars to spend and any leftover change as a result of finding more favorable prices was his to keep. In this way, he was saving up for a new bicycle.

The child is not simply exposed to the situation; rather, the child is prepared for the supermarket situation by being included in the planning of the purchases.

Certainly, the situation reported above describes a spectacular educational success, which probably occurs in this form (my child plans and executes the purchases) only very rarely. However, at the same time, it shows that next to reframing, participation in the situation is an important measure for avoiding derailments in routine situations. This technique can also prove valuable in other educational situations.

Here is what happens in the process: If you let your children or students participate, you are sharing responsibility with them. But, something else is also happening. You are not just giving them responsibility for planning and executing their own needs, but also trusting in them to care for the family needs. This can be an important opportunity for them to learn and practice social responsibility. If a child or adolescent feels that you have given them your trust, they can then attempt to fill a new role.

"LIFE" CHECKS IN DAILY SITUATIONS

Major educational concerns such as "educating for social participation and responsibility" must be achieved gradually, in small steps. It helps to shape routine situations—where possible—as educationally effective. This small effort requires no appeals, drum rolls, or policy statements, but, rather, can be established merely with attentiveness and a little fantasy.

By making a routine of this kind of parenting, you will take a major step towards effective education. You raise your children by living with them. For this reason, everyday situations that you experience with your children should always undergo a "life" check:

Let go: Try a fresh start! Do not let the familiar behavior of your child influence your expectations, fears, and responses! (Motto: "Everything could be completely different and it already is!")

Interpret slowly! Observe when and how you start to interpret: Think about whether you have an interpretation. Sit quietly in the corner and wait until this passes (de Shazer)! (Motto: "What image of my child do I always get?")

Fresh thoughts and actions: Examine and experiment! Try a contrast to the previous disputes and conflicts and practice alternative reactions! (Motto: "Today, I will reinvent myself as a father, mother, or teacher!")

Enable experience! Don't look for ways to avoid the demonstrated behavior of the other person; rather, ask yourself how you could prepare the upcoming situation as a new experience for your child or teenager! (Motto: "What educationally valuable lesson can my child learn without my saying too much about it?")

The aim of the LIFE principles for effective parenting is to change the way you relate to the child or adolescent. Parents, teachers, and those responsible for educating can no more bring about change in the child or teenager than a boss can change an employee. Rather, the basis of all change is a successful self-change (see Arnold 2010): As I change the way I see my child or student, they change themselves!

If you are frustrated, take time alone with your parenting principles and see the reflection in the mirror!

"It didn't do me any harm!" We often use these words when talking about what we experienced (or suffered) in our own upbringing. Sometimes we find ourselves reacting just like our parents did in certain situations. Sometimes educational opportunities escape us and we have to admit that we have overreacted. However, the soul of a child does not forget. The experience of an injustice or hardship leaves a trace—be it only a repressed memory, which then resurfaces, at the latest, when they are raising their own children.

> *As we repeat what we have experienced, we contribute, over the centuries, to the fact that much remains the same: cultures change more slowly than societies. Kingdoms crumble, but the parenting methods remain the same for centuries. Still, by reacting this way—which we consider intuitively justified—we are keeping true to tradition, but not focusing on the child.*

Fundamentally, there is also the self-fulfilling prophecy: If you do not believe in the potential of your child, you, after a time, will have a child that is unable to develop his potential. Teachers, who fear difficult or disruptive students, will continuously have to deal with such a child. It is our perception of others that determines the way we approach them. And the other person feels this.

Say good-bye to your principles and let the other person act on you. Try to understand what message they are trying to send to you through their behavior (which may often seem incomprehensible) and respond to that message.

LOOK INTO THE EDUCATIONAL MIRROR

Textbox 16.1

> In a teacher-training session, one teacher reported: "Well sometimes I am really disappointed in myself, especially, when I repeatedly flip out. I get loud and often unjust. Everything in me screams for a quick 'resolution'—a 'tit-for-tat' ending—and that is when I become exactly what I never wanted to be. In contrast, I wanted to do everything differently than I experienced myself as a child: abusive teachers, punitive parents, prohibitions everywhere—I myself never had a caring environment and I actually became a teacher to support my students, to talk with them, to make a meaningful experience possible. . . . But then Johnny acts up in class again, like last Monday in the sixth period, and I react in anger, even to myself a really unpleasant experience. And the worst thing about it: When I flip out like that, in just a few minutes, I destroy the basis of trust with my students that I have painstakingly developed over months!"

In such situations, you must look at your reflection in the educational mirror and gain an awareness of your inner thoughts and feelings about the topic of child rearing. If you are not aware of your inner voices and beliefs that always push their way to the fore to tell you what to do just when you are facing a stressful situation, then you are defenseless against them. You react in a way that feels justified or right deep within and, in such situations, you throw all your better instincts overboard. Your children or pupils then feel: "We knew it. When in doubt, we're always the ones that are wrong!"

> The educational mirror is a kind of rearview mirror that helps you to recognize the associations, images, and voices that catch up with you in certain situations. You can avoid being trapped in a corner by these familiar forms of thinking, feeling, and acting. You need to know that you are in control and can specify a new direction. The start of such a course change can happen, for example, when with the help of the following questions, you are able to identify what old acquaintances (feelings, interpretations, etc.) are trapping you and you greet them with the pat answer: "Too bad, I am no longer available!" (Jacobson 2009)

Table 16.1

The Educational Mirror: Looking for your inner parenting image!	
Feelings check	What feelings come to the surface? Paint these feelings into a picture!
Archeology	Where do you know these feelings from? Give them names (e.g., the Aunt Sally feeling) and sort out when they came upon you before!
Voice the attitude	Try to assign statements to each memory of a parenting situation (a key situation), e.g., "If you ever again . . .!"
Application	Where have these or similar feelings surfaced in your individual parenting reactions?
Voice of parenting wisdom	What would your parenting wisdom shout to these attitudes? Write these sentences down and assign them to the key situations!

The educational mirror can help us to more easily manage situations that press us and threaten to overwhelm us. As we learn to deal differently with our old emotions of anger, disappointment, or indignation, we give the child or adolescent the chance to show a new and different side.

Textbox 16.2

After we met with the teacher several weeks later, she had to admit—"the exercise with the educational mirror really changed some things! At the beginning, I was really skeptical and wondered: 'What is this all about? Am I the one responsible in the end for Johnny's behavior?' But after I looked in the mirror a few times with a colleague, I became more aware of why I freak out to that extent when Johnny again performs for his five minutes of fame. I always look at the picture of emotional landscape that I have painted and—you won't believe it—I recognize myself in this little fellow: Sometimes I use the same phrases that I had to listen to back in my wilder days. Since I have realized this, I flip out less often. It is much easier for me now to take another approach when a rule is broken and, for example, to respond according to the principle of 'no rule without consequence!' Johnny is still difficult every now and then, but he no longer makes such difficulties for me. Somehow, I have the impression that he gets himself under control even faster now."

The teacher provides an apt description of what actually happens in many parenting situations: We see ourselves before a difficult situation, but at the same time we feel an impulse within us to do something. When we follow this impulse, we are staying true to ourselves and our experiences. In other words, we react to a spontaneous assessment and follow our emotions. Only with deliberate hindsight, for example, obtained by using the educational mirror, will it become clear to us that our reaction is the same one we have always had in similar situations. We act according to the emotions welling up inside us, not to the way a more sober consideration of the situation would require.

> The more vehemently disappointment or annoyance rises in you from the "disturbing" behavior of your child or pupil, the more likely an old acquaintance is speaking up from within you. With the aid of the educational mirror, analyze the real meaning of the communication and spare the other person from having to experience the influence of your "old familiar friends"!

It is only with your ability to take a "sober" perspective of your children in an educational situation that you, as a parent or teacher, can act "reasonably." The child does not have the intention of violating your principles; he does not even know what these are. Children and teenagers behave the way they behave. They always have their reasons, even if they are not usually aware of this. By seeing only the violation of your educational principles and feeling your authority challenged, you are reacting based on your own measures, that is, "I undertake some action to make my world right for me." Although such a reaction is understandable, it is always educationally ineffective. Parenting achieves a long-term effect only when you can reach the world of the child and—at least for the moment—leave your own world of principles behind.

Never forget

It is not your child's behavior, but rather your interpretation of that behavior

This rule stems from the ancient Greek philosopher Epictetus, who stated in the first century: "The appearance of things to the mind is the standard of every action to man." This statement provides a basis for a new form of problem solving in the broad areas of education and parenting—the concept of "reframing" that is introduced in Rule 15. Literally, it means something like "placing something in a new frame." In other words, *we* have numerous educational conflicts simply because *we* are the ones who interpret the behavior of our children. We react based on a personal opinion, not on a rational assessment or on real contact with the child.

A great contribution to problem solving is made when you change your evaluation of the other person—not necessarily demanding a change in the other person.

PRACTICE SECOND-ORDER AWARENESS

In your educational reactions, if you can distance yourself from the idea that you can and must influence the reality of your children, you will be embarking on the path to a new, second-order awareness. This awareness is detached and more introspective. You are still annoyed about the experience, but in parallel, you can also observe your own anger and your own—often helpless—attempts at influencing the annoying behavior. At the same time, you will be attributing fundamentally less importance to the child's behavior.

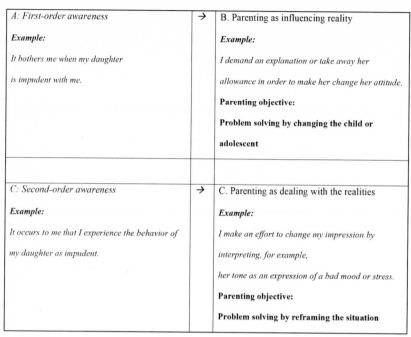

A: First-order awareness	→	B. Parenting as influencing reality
Example:		*Example:*
It bothers me when my daughter		*I demand an explanation or take away her*
is impudent with me.		*allowance in order to make her change her attitude.*
		Parenting objective:
		Problem solving by changing the child or
		adolescent
C: Second-order awareness	→	C. Parenting as dealing with the realities
Example:		*Example:*
It occurs to me that I experience the behavior of		*I make an effort to change my impression by*
my daughter as impudent.		*interpreting, for example,*
		her tone as an expression of a bad mood or stress.
		Parenting objective:
		Problem solving by reframing the situation

Figure 17.1

Parents and educators can exercise their second-order awareness. What is important is the realization that it is not the child's behavior that makes you think you have an "unreasonable" and "ill-tempered" child, but rather your interpretation of that behavior. Looking at the behavior in this way does not imply that you must approve of the form in which they present it. It is more about learning to observe yourself and pay attention to the words that you use to describe the disruptive behavior to yourself and to the other person.

TIPS FOR EFFECTIVE PARENTING

Two important lessons for effective parenting may be drawn from these examples:

(1) *Education is not always about immediate reactions and taking a position.* In many cases, it is this directness that leads to the battle lines being drawn and the issue coming down to who has the last word.

Textbox 17.1

In our example case, the mother says "My daughter gives me impudent answers and that aggravates me." The effort to look for a different interpretation of the daughter's irritating manner could change the situation entirely. A father answered: "When my daughter comes across as flippant, I have made good experience by simply keeping quiet. That is not quite correct: I really say to myself 'this has nothing to do with me!' and then give her a wide berth. Since I started doing it this way, I have had fewer difficulties with my daughter. Certainly, you still have to tell your children what is acceptable behavior and what is not. I do this when I am having a conversation with my daughter. It may happen that I say: 'Well, there is something else I want to say. Yesterday, I didn't like the way you spoke to me. Perhaps you were having a bad day or is something else bothering you?' As long as you give her the understanding that you are not taking it personally, she will not feel attacked and will be able to react calmly and with more understanding. Most importantly, I have made the experience that my education efforts are doomed to failure at the moment my daughter perceives them as an attack. Of course, it is really hard and it is not my job to treat my daughter carefully and with caution, but to give her feedback about her behavior and get her to change it, I have to be alert. My experience tells me that parents should be more calm and relaxed. You should not always react immediately, but rather hold your response until you are in a situation when your child will not feel attacked by your comments."

Such situations, where one word leads to another, are often the result of escalating emotions and the relationship between parents and children being damaged. Effective parenting depends on choosing the right time for the clarifications and explanations. Rarely does this time fall within the moment of annoyance.

Effective parenting does not consist of immediate reactions but rather in waiting for a suitable moment to explain, to clarify, or even to set boundaries. These moments will only happen if you are making eye contact with your child and she is listening to you and not experiencing your statements as attacks.

(2) *Education that has a lasting effect results from "the art of not tak-ing it personally."* This is easier said than done. I can already hear the voices saying to me: "That really takes the cake. My child is ranting at me and I should not take it personally? In that case, it won't be long before I am the laughingstock of my child!" This thought is understand-able, but it comes from a parental thinking that is based on enforcing standards, not achieving results.

> If your aim is to be effective, you must practice thinking and feeling like the other person. What matters is not whether you are right, but rather, whether you can cause an effect in the other person!

This orientation can be learned. Practice this three-level reflective thought process everyday:

Three levels of an effective educational response			
		Level 3	**I take advantage of a "favorable moment" to define the limits!** I do not forget the problematic conduct, but will bring it up later.
	Level 2		**I do not take it personally!** Introspection is demanded now: Observe how your anger shapes your judgments.
Level 1			**I watch, without reacting immediately!** It is useful to practice putting into words what you observe in the child's behavior choosing non-judgmental words (in the style of a short diary).

Figure 17.2

Practice the art of active listening! Ask questions that require thinking — not interrogations that support predetermined conclusions!

Child rearing is a form of developmental support. Parents or teachers support child development by spending time with them, by building a relationship with them, and by listening to their questions. It is fortunate when children come to us with their concerns and we should listen to them without giving in to the tempting urge "to storm into an answer" (Brunner-Peindl 2010, p. 17). Answers always provide something conclusive and guiding: If I give my child the answer, I take the responsibility away and it is no longer necessary for the child to discover his own answer.

An educationally effective question is one that is actually interested in the answers of the child and teenager. They are questions that we express to help them become aware of an issue and even answer on their own or find a solution for themselves.

Thomas Gordon, a respected American communication expert, emphasizes in many of his books that the foundation of educational communication is the capacity for "active" listening. When, as a father, as a mother, or as a teacher, you are able to communicate to the other person in a manner that causes them to get to the bottom of things on their own and be "clear" about things, you are actually contributing to the development of the child and to his becoming a responsible adult.

This conversation illustrates that it is not always about a clear solution or meaningful results. More important is the type of conversation. A topic was brought up in which the student determined the direction

Textbox 18.1

Student: You know I will graduate next spring and really do not want that. It would be great if I could stay in school for one more year.

Teacher: You are not happy about school ending.

Student: No, it is not really that I love school so much, it is that I do not have any idea about what to do next, you know? I want to continue at university, but that is so expensive and my father can't afford it. I could get a job, but the ones I could get offer low pay. There is not anything right for me.

Teacher: You sound pretty pessimistic about the options you have figured after graduation.

Student: Yes, I sure am, unless I was to go into the city where my friend lives and attend the art academy. I could live with him you understand. We would split the costs of the apartment, food, and such (*pause*). The problem is just that my father would kill me if he found out.

Teacher: You are afraid of how he would react if he learned that you are living with your boyfriend.

Student: Oh, I know how he would react. He would come and drag me back. That is another problem. My dad doesn't like Peter (that's my friend). Mainly that is because he has long hair and is crazy about music and art. Father is more of a strict type, you understand?

Teacher: They are very different?

Student: Not really. Underneath all his male posturing, my dad is very soft, similar to Peter . . . I think they are similar in many respects. It is just that my dad has very strong ideas about what a man has to do in order to be a real guy (. . .). He says Peter acts like a girl because he paints and composes and stuff like that.

Teacher: He believes that those things are not for boys?

Student: Yes, that is what he thinks (*pause*) I think he always wanted a boy (Gordon 1991, p. 75f).

while the teacher listened with interest. This highlights the "active" form of listening that not only reinforces the ability of the student to eventually make a decision on her own, but also develops a basis of trust between teacher and student that is of such educational significance that it should not be overlooked.

> Trust is the basis of all parenting success. Trust grows out of confidence and confidence is the reflection of the appreciation that we are able to express to our children and adolescents. In the words of the famous educator Rudolf Dreikurs: "Even a child needs evidence of your confidence." (Dreikurs/Blumenthal 2010, p. 370)

By actively listening to your children, you are trusting their view of things and believe that their way of identifying and mastering a problem is appropriate and ongoing. You limit yourself to the role of an interested, patient, and careful supporter. Decisive for the educational success of active listening is the trust in the process of developing a conversation. Gordon writes:

> The teachers must trust in the students to ultimately solve their own problems. If the student cannot quickly come to a solution, if they are verbose and vague and sound unconvinced . . ., then the teachers need to believe in the process and remember that active listening is there to facilitate the finding of solutions—a process, that may last days, weeks, even months. (ibid., p. 77)

Many parents as well as teachers have a difficult time learning how to guide this kind of confident conversation. Too pronounced are their impatience and their interest in quick solutions. As adults, they have long since forgotten all the detours and circular arguments that the search for an answer often requires. At a certain level, you must "become a child again"—as stated in the Bible, in order to truly accompany children effectively in their search. And, you must learn to ask thoughtful questions, not loaded questions.

Thoughtful questions are always open-ended questions. They open a door to educational effectiveness, whereas loaded questions tend to shut this door.

Thoughtful questions "taste like kisses" (Kindl-Beilfuß 2008). This means that effective educational questions are able to start something moving in the other person, just as a kiss is a mutual action if it is to "taste" (to stay with the same metaphor). Similarly there are also forced kisses that annoy us—just as a loaded question. Good questions, in contrast, stimulate the mind and mobilize an urge in the other person to think and share their thoughts with us. Ideally, questions can unsettle the other person and cause them to generate new thoughts, like how Socrates was able to accomplish in the squares of Athens: his questions showed people that they did not know, but rather just thought they knew, which made them question themselves—this is the core of his educational effect.

You can optimize your ability to listen actively and avoid asking loaded questions in your relationship with your children and students for whom you have educational responsibility. You may find it useful to ask the five questions from the following checklist:

Table 18.1

Am I an active listener for my child or my student
1. Can I accept the problem expressed by the child "as is" (Gordon) or do I catch myself thinking it cannot actually be as bad as they are saying?
2. Am I really in a position to develop this conversation or do my "answers" cause the other person to speak in monosyllables?
3. Do I really trust other persons, that is, do I believe they are capable of solving their own issues?
4. Do I treat the topic that the child or adolescent has told me about as confidential or do I gossip about it with other parents, teachers, etc.?
5. Am I confident that the other person says what is needed or expected of me, or do I always jump in and interrupt with controlling, directing, or absolute responses?

Always address every level of the child rearing problem!

As a rule, we describe a "disciplinary problem" as childhood or adolescent behavior that does not meet our expectations: an aggressive teenager disappoints our expectations of "appropriate" behavior just as much as the child who is completely closed and sits passively through class and breaks into tears if called on by the teacher. Often, parents, and those responsible for educating, end their efforts after an individual diagnosis, that is, they observe the "problematic" behavior as accurately as possible and examine whether and to what extent additional "clarification" might be helpful and, in effect, remain on the so-called first floor of diagnosis. Other insights into the mutually reinforcing conditions at the interpersonal, systemic, or even school-related dimensions of the situation in which the inappropriate behavior occurs are rarely discovered by those practicing educational development. This generally hinders any comprehensive clarification of the disciplinary problem, that is, across all floors. This dallying at the first level of problem analysis is insufficient because:

> Frequently, the extent of the behavioral problem cannot be explained adequately on a personal level. Individual learning disabilities, e.g., reading and writing weaknesses only become a hindrance to development following inappropriate reactions by the school or family. (Hennig/ Knödler 2000, p. 270)

Always consider all dimensions of an educational problem. Although this is observed in the conduct of the child or adolescent, it may first become a problem due to conditions or reactions on other "floors." This implies that modifications or changes on the other floors can contribute to the minimization or even the elimination of problems on another floor.

				Multi-dimensional Questions
			Fourth Floor: School macro-system	(10) What are the general characteristics of the school that may have a favorable/disturbing effect?
				(9) What administrative roles and expectations have a favorable/disturbing effect?
		Third Floor: System level		(8) What function does the disruptive behavior take on in terms of the class? What is gained from this?
				(7) How can the class be included in the solution to the problem?
	Second Floor: Interpersonal level			(6) What is the teacher response to the disruptive conduct? What is your relationship to the child or adolescent?
				(5) How does the class deal with this offending behavior?
				(4) Is there a time (situation) when the offending behavior is not present? What is different in these situations?
First Floor: Personal level				(3) How is the individual behavioral problem being outwardly expressed?
				(2) How does the person describe and explain the behavior or problem?
				(1) Are there any indications of a physical disorder, an attention disorder syndrome (ADHS) or hyperactivity?

Figure 19.1

The passage through this systemic floor model for the analysis of educational problems can help to make things easier for the parties. Many times, creating favorable conditions on a higher floor can facilitate things to remain the same on one of the "lower" floors. For this

Textbox 19.1

"Claudio is annoying!" This was the opinion of many of the 7C teachers at a teachers' meeting: Things cannot continue this way with Claudio. "He just cannot sit still in class. He repeatedly gets up and goes over to a classmate and when I warn him, he just grins at me and keeps on doing it. If you ask me, his academic performance also suffers because of this lack of concentration!" said one teacher. "Yes I am concerned about Claudio's grades. He rarely does the homework I assign and I notice that he does not have any real friends. Some even tease him because he is a bit slow. Recently, I invited his parents to come in for a meeting, but only his grandfather showed up. He quickly indicated that from now on Claudio 'would dance to a different tune' as he phrased it. If you ask me, that had little effect. Since then, Claudio has actually gotten more agitated and rarely has any concentration at all."

reason, when confronted with a specific problem, you should always make the effort to visit the trouble spots on all floors from bottom up and from top down. Before you initiate complicated modifications on a lower floor, ensure that "everything is OK" on the upper floors.

An examination by the school psychologist revealed that Claudio possessed an above-average intelligence and did not suffer from any physically based concentration disorders. At a two-hour meeting with the psychologist, Claudio came across as a "bright boy," capable of holding a factual conversation. When asked about the problem, he stated: "It is like this. Everyone wants something from me and I get all confused and feel a great urge to get up and walk around!"

The systematic walk-through of the floors for an explanation to the "disciplinary problem" brought to light some aspects which had not been previously considered by the teachers:

Textbox 19.2

The school psychologist, who attended several classroom sessions, noted that the teachers already looked at Claudio through the "disturbance lens," as he expressed it. Asked what he meant by this, he answered: "I observed that you—to be blunt about it—only look at Claudio when he is disturbing the class, for example, causing interference by walking around. Claudio has internalized the lesson: I get attention when I create a disturbance!" "Hey, come on, talk is cheap," said one rather indignant teacher. "We cannot simply let him walk around!" The psychologist added, "I didn't mean that at all, but still you should pay attention to how you deal with Claudio. What do you do when he is not interfering, what happens then? Yesterday during geography class, for example, I saw Mr. Kline call on Claudio and when he answered correctly, the teacher praised him and asked him to walk up to the chalkboard and write down his solution. My suggestion is: Approach Claudio directly at the times when he is behaving well and put him in motion! You will see that this type of attention is much more to his liking. And another thing: Pay attention to his classmates' reaction. The next time he seeks

(cont...)

Textbox 19.2 *(cont...)*

attention by disrupting the class, simply go towards him, touch his shoulder, and walk him back to his seat—without making any comment regarding his behavior. Simply continue teaching your class and pay no more attention to the interruption."

This information led the participants away from the first floor of the problem analysis to another floor. In the process, they realized not only that "disturbances" are a form of individual misbehavior, but also that they can be either reinforced or constrained by the manner in which the environment deals with them. The walk-through of the floors strengthened the solution perspective of those responsible and they learned, among other things, to focus less on the problematic behavior and more on creating situations in which it no longer occurs, and the "difficult student" is not really all that difficult.

Use the BARE essentials: Bonding, Active involvement, Respect for boundaries, and Education!

Parents are always asking for ideas about how to raise a child. They hope to find a kind of general guidance, appropriate and effective, as a response to their children. However, long gone are the times in which such an orientation was determined by the church or the society. Today, only charlatans try to preach such ideas, for example, "discipline must be enforced at any cost," as the panacea for all educational problems or the current antipampering programs according to the motto "Challenge, don't spoil!" The disadvantage of such general concepts is that they don't work in all cases, and they are accompanied by considerable risk and side effects. Frequently, such ideas regarding the behavior of children and teenagers are the cause of major problems for the parents, the teachers, and the society.

Beware of self-help parenting guides that suggest all difficulties that you may have with your children or students can be resolved by a pat formula. All children are not the same. That is why we need various educational measures. Successful parents and teachers have a wide range of strategies and reactions and they know about the helplessness and ineffectiveness of "louder" and "more resolute" educational advice.

There is no one prerequisite for a long-term effective education, but rather, there are many! Most important among them are: the *clarity of mind of those responsible* and the *relationship to the developing child*. This means that an effective education is next to impossible if clarity is not established. Children and teenagers must be able to understand what you expect from them, and they also need to understand what the consequences are for behavior that violates clearly communicated limits.

Textbox 20.1

In a popular TV show with the title "The strictest parents in the world" (see www.kabeleins.de), there is an episode in which German parents are unable to cope with the behavior of their teenage children, and they send them to live with Romanian parents for a kind of "educational holiday." Once there, the children are confronted with clear rules and tasks and they are also expected to work on the farm. The host parents are loving and open, but also strict. They confront the adolescents with clear rules and throw them out if they disregard these rules—a hard, but in this specific case, effective consequence: left with no money, the teenagers don't get far and are forced to ruefully return to the host parents. However, getting to this point cost them a great deal of inner pain and soul searching as they experienced that they had come to the end of their options. They had no other choice and had to come to terms—yielding, yet accompanied by key insights into the fragilities associated with the life they had experienced before.

THE ELEMENTS OF CHILD REARING

This case illustrates what elements—as in a kinetic mobile—must be present at the same time so that education can be successful:

Bonding: Interest in growth and development

Announcing and enforcing the limits is not an attempt to prove that the host parents are right. Rather, they link the experience of getting kicked out ("I cannot survive here alone") with their intention to give the teenagers an insight, without which they would not be able to develop into mature adults. It is this interest in the growth of the other person that makes a consequence an effective educational experience, not the consequence for the sake of consequence.

If you respond by enforcing a consequence, always ask yourself what is the significance of this experience on the growth and development of the child or adolescent. Disciplinary consequences should result in the child or adolescent gaining some new insight. Avoid consequences from which nothing is learned! Ensure that the consequences of disciplining your child can be reasonably expected to provide an important experience—even an unpleasant one!

Active Involvement: *Restrained, but present*

Parents and educators are faced with the difficult task of constantly maintaining a balance between security on the one hand and confinement on the other. Again and again, they must question whether their educational responses are still within the balance of a restrained but present leadership or, have they "drifted" into the more familiar waters of a confining style of education. The suction in the direction of these waters is great and it always leads ultimately to the fact that

> many of us educate our children no differently than the way our forefathers had practiced for hundreds of years: according to reward and punishment. But—even if you have not thought about this—the system is based on the assumption that the child is unreasonable, stupid, unreliable, and an inferior being, not to be tamed without threats and bribery. And this is precisely the parenting method that most parents still subscribe to this day! While this may have worked in earlier times—today it is no longer successful because it does not correspond to the societal conditions of a modern democracy. (Dreikurs/Blumenthal 2010, p. 19f)

Respect for Boundaries: *Forming attachments, not fences*

The consequences enforced by the host parents in our example may appear harsh, and biological parents cannot simply kick their children out of the house. But, they have other measures at their disposal by which they can translate their words into actions. This harshness that your children may feel does not come from an aggressive intent, but rather from the raw reality governed by different standards than those of continuous protection and constant leniency. Indulgence and protection can be a subtle form of confinement that deprives the adolescent of important experiences that are necessary for him to mature.

If care turns into overprotection, you are depriving the child of a world of experiences. This confinement can be harmful as the child loses the opportunity to learn and feel what self-responsibility means in life.

The rough reality can only be experienced, not explained. That is why children and, especially, teenagers must be allowed to experience serious situations, where they are exposed to this reality. At the same time, they must feel there is always a safe harbor for them to return to after these first "tentative steps." Through such experiences, they feel socially "attached."

The basis of all educational success is affection and appreciation. This is the connection to the expression: It is all about caring limits, not limiting care.

Education: *The higher development of the self*

Education has the ultimate goal of contributing to the higher development of the child. In other words, it helps the child to develop a more self-managed and contributory personality and to become a more and more mature individual. Parenting contributes to this development.

In the absence of any of the above prerequisites (bonding, active involvement, respect for boundaries, education) the self-expression of the adolescent will sometimes seek a winding, but also a desperate, path. Disciplinary problems usually refer to a shortcoming in one of the BARE essentials. Parenting excesses are attempts to dispose of the "pent-up emotions" (Alice Miller) of those responsible for education— sometimes with devastating effects on the growth and development of the individual as well as the social fabric of the shared lives.

Make your child the center of attention from time to time! Love is vital!

Although they are still trying to find themselves, children and teenagers have a life story that has made them the persons they are. Consequently, the basis for a long-term education is to recognize the child or teenager as an individual, not just as an unfinished being, still evolving. Generally, parents and teachers already have a more or less finished picture of the child or adolescent opposite them and this limits the view and prevents the other individuals from being able to show themselves in the way they want. The VITAL exercise helps parents and teachers to focus an open and loving gaze on the individual:

> Often, it is our limited view of the other person that provides the reality, which then annoys or upsets us. If you constantly observe your child as a (still) unfinished product, you should not wonder if your child's true appearance escapes you. As a father, mother, or teacher, opening your loving gaze on the other person allows them to change because you now see them in a different light. Therefore, always let your child become the subject of your observation and center of your attention!

This vital "focusing of your gaze" is a silent exercise that places your child at the center of attention. It can be practiced alone or in the company of parents who do not know what to do, or by a teacher who "suffers" under a "difficult" student. By rethinking your view of the child or adolescent and following the signs to help you open your view, the picture you have carried around with you will start to change. The new and altered image in your heart makes you capable of responding differently, by not placing too much weight on certain behaviors and taking a more positive view of the individual's overall education.

Table 21.1

	Take a vital look at your children or students
Vitality	*When do I feel most alive with my child?* This refers to the quiet moments when you look at your child and feel that this being will produce something new and unique (new questions, ideas, contributions, etc.). Parents also know the feeling that their own vitality somehow lives on in their children, continuing beyond their own lives.
Identity	*How is this child different from others?* As I look at my child's uniqueness, I meet with his identity. This special potential and talent becomes visible, which escapes me when I look at my child only through the lens of performance and good conduct, because that look focuses on the deficits, discrepancies, and the "not yets."
Talent	*What is this child particularly good at doing?* Every person has special abilities and talents. I am aware of the fact that talents are not "had" but are "gifted." That is the reason I struggle to "endow" my child with talents by appreciating his special abilities.
Appearance	*How does this child move me and others?* Everyone acts and affects by his spontaneous In-The-World feeling. How does my child affect me? What will I learn from his manner and behavior? What picture of him do I keep close to me? How does this image alter me? Can I start to see my child differently and with new eyes?
Learning	*How has this child developed over the last 2–3 years?* My impatience and everyday stress lead me to overlook all that my child has learned in recent months and years. I try to take the time, to notice my child, and to be more aware of the progress in his development.

Textbox 21.1

During a meeting of parents, one father reported: "OK, at first I didn't want to go through these questions. Somehow I felt, 'What good will it do? My boy has not earned such a loving gaze from me, after all he expects from us.' But then it was somehow moving to suddenly get this warm feeling and I also had to think about how I was as a small boy. To be honest, I gave my parents many a sleepless night. And the best was as I thought about all the special things about my son. Suddenly the problem that I came here to talk about and solve had lost its importance and I felt a load being lifted—along the lines:

(cont...)

Textbox 21.1 *(cont...)*

'Man, living with kids can be difficult at times, but I wouldn't want to be without my children.' When I got home, my son had somehow changed. I thought he felt that I was interested in him and he demonstrated a whole new side to himself. Or, perhaps, it is just that up until now, I had been overlooking so much in him because I always cared only about whether he was doing things right. If I am honest, deep inside I always figured that he would leave the lights on at night again, staying up half the night in front of his PC, or wake up too late in the morning. . . . And, whether you believe me or not, since I started paying attention to other things, this hardly happens anymore. That is somehow eerie!"

There is nothing mystical about this effect. It is understandable that children and teenagers need our love. In their searching way, they can feel if and how we are looking at them and then act accordingly, in a way that makes them visible to us. By the way we choose to look at them, we can open the curtains to a stage on which they can appear, just as we can close the curtains. Consequently, a "difficult" student usually has no chance of appearing other than through the curtain of disturbance, because that is how we have set our gaze. In effect, our hidden fears create exactly what we are afraid of—an effect known in communication theory as the "self-fulfilling prophecy."

LEARN TO TURN THE TABLES

The effect of the "self-fulfilling prophecy" is that parents and teachers sometimes unintentionally support precisely that behavior they are trying to change. The mechanism that takes effect is the following: That which I fear only occurs because I am expecting it from deep within my heart. If you understand this effect, you can use it to your advantage by turning the tables.

The former fear becomes obsolete, that is, superfluous. Austrian philosopher Ludwig Wittgenstein, who also identified this mechanism for changing the reality, wrote:

How is it that the new makes the old obsolete?—We have seen something else and can no longer play naïve. (Wittgenstein 1956, p. 100)

Parents as well as teachers can practice turning the tables. In the end, it is all about switching from the old to the new form of dealing with a problematic situation.

Table 21.2

Exercise: Turning the tables	
The Old	The New
What bothers you most about your child's behavior?	Imagine a situation when you were totally satisfied with what your child did!
Imagine your child could not help it, because there is just something about her and she can do nothing about it!	Take the annoying behavior for just what it is: An impulse my child follows for reasons I do not understand, but also are not deliberately chosen.
Watch yourself: When does your anger start and what exactly are you angry about?	Before you express your anger: Recall a situation of joy with your child! Look at the disturbing situation through this picture!
Write down your actual disappointment in one sentence (e.g., "I am sad and disappointed that my child lied to me!").	Try to add another positive thought to the sentence (e.g., ". . . my child lied to me, but nevertheless, can still behave lovingly!").

If you can learn to deal differently with an annoying situation, the situation changes because your gaze is on your child as a whole in the center of attention, and not on the behavior that is annoying you!

When parents and teachers use a new gaze when looking at children or adolescents, the annoying situation loses much of its previous character. Suddenly, the gaze is on the child, not (only) on the behavior. Consequently, new paths to a solution can be identified and traveled together.

Improve the hidden influences in your child's learning environment!

Children and teenagers develop their personality and their abilities not from instructions, but by the stimuli that come from the environment. This environment is a world shaped and influenced by adults. It is a place where father, mother, or significant other, as well as the teachers and educators, hold privileged positions owing to the fact that the children and adolescents live and interact with them. Children watch and imitate the behavior of these relevant adults and the adolescents begin to rely on the growing influence of their circle of friends—it is from this hidden curriculum of life that children and adolescents get their orientation and patterns of behavior for their own development.

Textbox 22.1

One mother reported about her 23-year-old son: "Kevin is so much like my husband. Their voices are even quite similar if you could hear them speak. When I discuss something with him and he wants to have it his way, he has the same combination of charm and persistence that I have always admired in his father. The similarity is really amazing! At the same time, I also notice Kevin is often still rather unsure of himself. If he is scolded for something, it is always really bad for him, as if he feels no longer loved. Suddenly, that is the end of the cool behavior and I sense very clearly that he is still just a boy."

Many parents are familiar with these and similar impressions. These impressions show us how we influence our children, simply by being the way we are—without being aware of it. The effect is unavoidable and we can only influence it by observing how we set up the *hidden curriculum* to which our children are exposed.

Long-lasting education focuses increasingly less attention on explicit instructions, warnings, or guidance (motto: "How can I tell that to my child?"), and rather, relies more on indirect messaging and behavioral areas where children and teenagers can participate and help in shaping a shared experience (motto: "What do I show my children by the way I interact with them?").

What do I show my children by the way I interact with them?				
Dimensions of a long lasting, hidden education	I ensure that may children or students …	Often	Rarely	Never
Naturalness	… have a natural and trusting relationship with each other. … can observe an open way of dealing with conflict and seeking solutions. … find room for mutual experience.			
Prevent fear	… learn to express their fears and anxieties. … feel how helpful it is to trust another person. … never get into a frightening situation because of me.			
Warmth	… open their hearts and trust to me. … can see me as a person and come into touch with me. … see and feel my joy of life.			
Authenticity	… can see how I really think and feel. … can appreciate what makes me happy or annoys me. … can feel my genuine interest in what moves and interests them.			

Figure 22.1

After your honest and self-critical review of these or similar questions concerning the learning environment that you, as a father, mother, or teacher, create for the child or adolescent, you should be able to improve the hidden effects that emanate from this environment. This is especially necessary if you assessed one or more of the dimensions as being "rarely" or "never" satisfied. The most important impulses for experience and development do not come from the explicit (admonitions, declarations, etc.), rather from these interactive experiences.

80 percent of long-lasting education derives from the way you act around your children or adolescents when you are not teaching them. It is the naturalness and prevention of fear as much as the warmth and authenticity that creates the framework in which your child can explore and develop. The real educational effects are generated through this frame—the indirect educational effects.

WAYS TO ESTABLISH PARENTAL CLOSENESS

If you recognize that this framework is only partially developed, you should make a deliberate effort to modify the subject areas. The proposals below may assist you in this effort:

Table 22.1

	Ways to establish parental closeness
Naturalness	• Create situations in which you just horse around with your children!
	• Let your children be a part of what brings you enjoyment (hobbies etc.)!
	• Show your children how you enjoy and master your life!
	• Let them participate in how you deal with your anger or conflicts!
	• Give your children confidence in an everyday life so they can feel how important they are!
Prevent fear	• Show your children that you can also be afraid, but that you know ways to beat it!
	• Devote yourself to the worries and fears of your children, without wanting to downplay or dismiss their feelings!
	• Avoid threats and situations in which your children do not know what is going to happen to them!
Warmth	• Express your love, appreciation, and happiness to other people, because children learn not only from the attention you give them, but also from what you give to others!
	• Think that in all your reactions to your children, how much their growth and well-being mean to you!
	• Let your children experience the relationship by listening and giving them time and encouragement!
Authenticity	• Show your child how you deal with your mistakes!
	• Tell your child things about yourself and your life!
	• Show them that life is full of new requirements and also disappointments, which are just waiting to be overcome!

By deliberately trying to change the hidden curriculum experienced by your children simply because they live with you, observe you, have a relationship with you, seek and find a sense of belonging, you will land in the indirect educational effect. *You design and improve the soil for a fertile education.* In this context, many books about education talk of education as "A Thoughtful Classroom Program" (Callo 2002, p. 22). This program acts through professional precautions or interventions only to a lesser extent; its actual effect is more informal. We educate just when we are not aware of it and we educate by the way we design the daily life that our children also experience. This is true, in particular, for the design of school life, because it is mostly determined by administrative requirements, whereby the students learn—secretly learn—that learning is an event that you must comply with, not an activity where you can spontaneously express your life energy. In school, children and adolescents not only learn what we expect, but, frequently, also acquire a "learned helplessness" according to the motto: "We learn not for real life, but for school!"—A fateful lesson for a learning society.

Give your children some space
A little distance can bring you even closer!

Raising children also means watching and considering them from a distance, because "parenting lives from distance *and* closeness!" Many parents find this rule difficult. In their educational approach, they unconsciously follow an ideal of closeness, which may lead to a total lack of detachment to their children, a situation in which effective education is no longer possible. When there is no detachment in your devotion to another person, you are predisposed to accept them as they are and you will try to support them and accompany their forms of expression. This is what Erich Fromm describes in his book *Die Kunst des Liebens* (see Fromm 2000) as the core of all love. However, this love is only one part of the love that flows between parents and children. Parental love is always an expression of vicarious responsibility. Parents actively try to take care of the child's future. They know their child is expressing what is inside them through their behavior, but they also know that this form of expression is part of their search.

However, this concern requires a detached perspective of your child. If you are too closely attached to your child and, at the same time, not able to take a detached view, there is the danger of putting your child on a pedestal and of ultimately accepting their views: Never questioning the actions of the child or placing them in the broader context of life's responsibilities. Such pampering and elevated attitudes are often observed in single-child families or even the single-parent households. Finally, this exaggerated closeness and protection impairs the child's chances to develop. By insulating your children from the "harsh reality" and not exposing them to detached experiences, you are failing to adequately prepare them for the real world.

PRACTICE THE DETACHED VIEW

Practice the detached view of your child! Ask yourself if you can see things with realistic eyes. Use the perceptions and comments of others to give yourself a better picture of the possibilities and limitations of your child! You can only lend positive support to the development of your child if you have such help!

Table 23.1

Close	Detached
My children trust me. They share and I listen. I understand their searching ways. (Motto: "Speak with me, I am always there for you!")	I observe and see my child through the eyes of another. Then I notice their tendencies for pretension, exaggeration, and self-estimation as they go about their lives. (Motto: "I'll tell you what I expect of you!")

Closeness-Distance Balance
I usually manage to find the balance between closeness and distance. I provide my children a framework of trust, which gives them the feeling of generally being supported and loved in all their actions. But then, I also clearly tell my children what I expect from them and I do not believe in mincing my words and beating around the bush.

Textbox 23.1

A single parent and mother of four children reported that she had a special inner connection with her youngest. She had raised him for many years by herself and developed a kind of routine togetherness, which led to the fact that the aspect of closeness in their relationship was very subtle and deeply developed. In an interview, referring to her son, she said that the two of them could, in her words, "hear the grass growing in the other's soul" and that you "can't slide a sheet of paper between us." As her son, who meanwhile had turned 20-years old, began to distance himself from her with his shrill and self-centered thoughtlessness, she went to see a child guidance agency. The counselor pricked up his ears at such formulations and

(cont...)

Textbox 23.1 *(cont...)*

showed her how to practice being a detached parent. He said, "If you stand in the middle of the woods, you can't see the forest through the trees! But, as a parent you have to distance yourself from your son and consider the overview. Only with some detachment, will the closeness to your son have the power to develop as you would like."

Effective parenting requires both closeness and detachment. If you are standing too close, you can't see the actual movements of your children and because of this you are often not close to them at all.

An important topic in this context is the question as to what position the child actually takes toward the parent. Again and again, this question highlights the same mistake made by many parents: you make a quasi-equal place "at your side" for your son or daughter—an arrangement that can lead to confusion in their souls.

Systemic family therapy works frequently with family pictures that show the parents next to each other on one level and—from some distance—gaze at their children, who are standing side by side before them. This pose is, of course, an inner picture, which nevertheless expresses the way a family is organized in the hearts of the family members. Often, this is not the same picture that children sketch of their parents on a different level. It may be that the son is internally very close to his mother, her confidant and partner in conversation, whereas the father is seen as more detached from events. There are also many cases where the daughter is very close to the father and is his pride and joy, while the wife is standing at a distance and observing the events. Such alliances between a child and one parent often leave so much in disarray—especially in the souls of the children. They experience their father or mother as needy and feel responsible for their happiness or even their comfort, whereby they land on a level almost on a par with the parents. There are other cases, where one parent finds their position close to their partner somehow already "filled." Due to the constellation of inner images they must occupy the position of a child: for example, the father is cautioned by the son because, in his inner picture of the family situation, he does not really know who he is and what position he should occupy.

Make sure your own family relationships "match," i.e., never mix up the pictures of the parents' relationship to each other with the relationship to the children. This is the foundation required for effective parenting. Disciplinary measures do not really work if children do not have a sense of their own position. A prerequisite for education is the establishment of some distance between the parent and the child or adolescent.

Textbox 23.2

In a patchwork family, the new husband is never really capable of taking a parental position in relation to the adolescent son from her first marriage. "The two of them are like a secret society. If I try to reprimand or even have a serious word with him, you can bet that I will soon have a conflict with my wife, who defends her son and accuses me of having something against her son. If you want my opinion, there is a lot of confusion in that boy's mind. That is why he lets himself go and, again and again, comes across to me as stupid. Meanwhile, I have given up and am just waiting for the problem to go away in three years when he has graduated."

CHECK YOUR OWN BEHAVIOR

Checklist to assess your own ability for detached parenting			
Question	*Often*	*Rarely*	*Never*
I often tell my child what I actually expect and what I think of their behavior.			
I put up a united front with my partner when he or she has a disciplinary issue with my child.			
I do not allow my child to "wrap me around his finger."			
I listen with an open mind if another person (e.g., teacher) offers a justified criticism of my child and I calmly seek an explanation.			
I am consequential when it comes to my disciplinary measures.			
I can have my child talk respectfully with me and my partner.			
I intervene when my child gets out of line and is unappreciative.			

Figure 23.1

This checklist is designed to help monitor your own behavior in the parenting role for the child you love and for whom you are responsible. Use all "Rarely" or "Never" responses to see the areas where more can be done to clarify the relationships to your children. Your parenting success is often based, to a large degree, on the clarity of these relationships!

Teach your child self-discipline by looking beyond your own fears and idealistic views!

Education is based on the experiences that we provide our children and adolescents. For this reason, self-discipline, self-reliance, and self-responsibility can develop only if we let them have such experiences. Keeping your children "on a tight leash" or even bullying them will not work. This insight is the winning argument against all possible forms of disciplinary action as they are proposed in so many books on parenting. "Self-discipline is acquired through freedom, not through discipline" (Arnold 2007, p. 4). Discipline tends rather towards escalation, and although it offers parents and those responsible for education the opportunity, as mentioned earlier, to dispose of "pent-up emotions" (Alice Miller), it often impairs the trust of the children and adolescents. In just a fraction of a second, we can destroy the bridges to a relationship with our children, which took us years to build.

Always remember: Disciplinary escalation (yelling, chewing out, punishing, etc.) serves as a vent for your own aggression more than for any educational purpose. When you cause a temporary intimidation of the opponent, not only are you frighteningly ineffective, but also, you are very quickly able to destroy the threads that hold a relationship together, which you needed years to knit. Anxiety, threats, and intimidation also destroy the fabric that all successful education is made of: the one called "I am OK and I can make a difference!"

Textbox 24.1

The parents reported increasing difficulties that have been confronting them in recent months regarding their adolescent son, Manuel: "Well, this is all very discouraging for us. Previously, Manuel would take part in our family life, today he hides out in his room and, if he has to help in the household, he usually ignores our requests or spits poison at us saying something to the effect that we should leave him alone!"—reported the father. The mother added with a sad look: "Sometimes I wonder where my boy has gone. This teenager who comes and goes from our home is nothing at all like the sweet and tender child he used to be!"

The disappointment of these parents is clearly evident in this example. The counselor's question, "Could it be that Manuel is merely defining himself and trying to grow up?" produced only a resigned nod of their heads. Still, the counselor continued with his questions:

Textbox 24.2

"Could it be that you are trying to hold on to an image of your son and this image is standing in the way of you and your son and damaging the relationship?"—"Now we are expected to accept the blame for the whole quarrel?"—replied the irritated father. "No, but often it is like this. It is difficult for the parents to understand that the child is finding its own way. In my experience, I can say the more 'sweet' and 'tender' they were as small children, to use your own words, the harder this defining process is"

If something has disappointed you, observe what pictures of your child you carry in your heart, and try to figure out what picture your child is trying to express.

"IMAGE SEARCH" EXERCISE

This image search exercise consists of three steps. In effect, it will reveal the idealization of your own child. This is common since almost all parents carry an internal picture of "their child." It is rare when they are aware of the fact that this makes it difficult for them to have an adequate gaze when the child's behavior is different. You are looking to a certain extent through your own idealized images, and therefore, you are unable to consider them without simultaneously evaluating them. However, because of this, a vicious cycle is set in motion: the parents do not see the child, but merely the deviations from their idealistic image and this misunderstanding, in turn, leads to the fact that the child now feels "invisible" and retreats more and more inwardly, which is further seen by the parents as a painful deviation—consequently, a vicious circle of mutual disappointments.

Table 24.1

Image search or: Ten questions for "de-imaging"		
Parenting images that cause "the problem" to arise	Questions	Risks and side effects
My ideal ("my boy," "my girl") Lesson A: *"What really bothers me"*	• Collect adjectives that describe your expectations of your perfect child. • Describe your vision of how your child will be living in ten years.	• What are you doing unintentionally to your child, when you measure him or her against your perfect picture? • How does this make your child feel when he or she senses this?
My fear Lesson B: *"My fear is primarily for me"*	• What are you afraid of (a) for yourself and (b) for the child if the "problem behavior" persists? • Paint a picture of doom. (Ask: "What will become of him or her if this continues?")	• Who or what feeds your fears and what do these actually have to do with your child?
Their ideal image Lesson C: *"Every differentiation is a "no" to what has gone before."*	• Use non-judgmental words to describe what your child is striving for right now. • How does the child picture life in ten years?	• Do I welcome these ideas or denigrate them in my inner monologs and the way I talk about them with my child?

Education does not succeed, as those responsible for education want to believe, as a result of their own conditions, but rather exclusively because of the interaction with the conditions of the child or adolescent. Parents and teachers must therefore track down and recognize how their own idealizations or even dogmas ("That is not nice") hinder or prevent their educational effectiveness. Only if we try to understand the child or adolescent from their own actions can we hope to accompany and support them.

Textbox 24.3

"The image search exercise was really hard for me. I had the feeling at first that I had to throw away many of my own ideas and expectations, before I could even start to consider what was motivating my son," said Manuel's father, who was asked to complete the image exercise whenever he thought his son's behavior was fully inconceivable and impossible. "It is truly strange that I had to throw out so much in order to become more effective. Today, I realize that all discipline is self-discipline and I have learned to observe my son's development—without immediately judging. It was surprising to me to find out that I suddenly found new interest in what he was thinking and doing—a wonderful experience."

The father expresses what research tells us: You cannot really raise children—without risks and side effects—we can only monitor and support their self-development.

We are able to support only after we have successfully, as educators, processed these three lessons: "What really bothers me," "My fear is primarily for me," and "Each differentiation is a 'no' to what has gone before." These help us to change our understanding of parenting: We no longer recognize it as a contracted duty that we must (and can) perform, but as an opportunity to accompany children and teenagers along their road to self-development.

Avoid going down the "dead ends" of child rearing!

Educational research concludes that direct education, through warnings, punishment, or talks, etc., has an uncertain effect, and of even greater concern, it is not free of risk and side effects. This means that it is difficult to predict how a direct or confrontational disciplinary measure will work, obviously, because too many other conditions also play a determining role. You can try to account for these framework conditions, but the only way to increase the likelihood that a disciplinary measure will be effective is to practice.

It matters, for example,

- whether the disciplinary intervention occurs directly following the offensive behavior or later in the evening (when father is home): *The chance of effectiveness is zero if the reaction is late and comes through an intermediary;*
- what tone is used and what are the gestures when you address the child or adolescent: *The receptivity of the child or adolescent is shut down by relationship-ending and "abusive" tones;*
- whether the reaction seems genuine and actually leads to a consequential behavior or merely takes the form of a notice: *Announced consequences are blunt disciplinary measures;* and
- whether the "relationship remains intact" and things are "good" after the disciplinary measures: *Resentment is not educational.*

PRACTICE YOUR EXITS

Define and exercise your escape routes from the ineffective dead ends of parenting behavior by using the summary below:

Table 25.1

Disciplinary dead ends	Exit	Exercise
The **"Wait till your father gets home" reaction** *The chances of being effective are zero if you react late and through an intermediary*	**Self-discipline lasts longer!** We create the relationship to our children through discipline; consequently, discipline should not be delegated or deferred.	(1) Practice the principle "Discuss offenses immediately!" Use such talks to clearly state what is bothering you and what you are going to do! (2) Only you can express what annoys you (in your child's behavior). You may not transfer this responsibility to another!
The **"You are bad" reaction** *Relationship-ending and "abusive" tones close the child's or adolescent's receptiveness*	**You challenge me!** Children test themselves and us. Can you really blame them for that? Work with clear if-then rules and enforce them!	(3) Practice avoiding any opinionated and denigrating comments of the experienced behavior. Share your appraisal. Explain your views with if-then statements. Say what is unacceptable to you and act accordingly.
The **ridiculous threat** *Announced disciplinary measures are blunt instruments*	**Don't talk, act!** Children want to believe what you say to them. Think: You can only be not credible three times, after that you are ridiculous!	(4) The effectiveness of disciplinary action "thrives" on your credibility. Sometimes it is better to be silent than to say something that you cannot enforce. Practice binding talks!
The **"Sulky parent"** *Resentful behavior is not parenting*	**I am grown up, you are not!** Sulking is not an adult emotion. By entering into this childish feeling, you lose much of your authority and are no longer on the level of adults!	(5) Carefully observe whether the frustrations and provocations of your children are "solved" by talking or whether you are still resentful. Practice objectivity in your discipline!

Textbox 25.1

The reaction of one father to such suggestions illustrates how difficult it is to avoid the dead end of ineffectiveness. "What is that supposed to mean? 'Objectification of discipline?' If my child lies to me, I will be angry and at that moment, I will have no desire to continue speaking with him/her!" The counselor understood this response very well, reflecting that it is the same at his home. "But you must understand that turning away in anger is ineffective from an educational point of view." He added, "Something else is involved: If you 'stew about it,' then you are depriving your child of an important educational experience, which you could express in words as: 'If I have disappointed my father, he will say something to me and explain to me what consequences I should expect, but he still loves me!' You cannot imagine how important it is to differentiate between your 'sobering disappointment' and the relationship you have with your child, which you do not really want to terminate. As parents, we always are in a relationship with our children and we should not act in a behavioral conflict as though we can terminate it. Of course, it is easier to sulk and distance yourself from his or her behavior than to keep up the exchange with your child. I know that too, but that is precisely what we must learn to do if we are to become more effective parents."

THE QUESTION OF GUILT

Ultimately, it comes down to a question of *guilt or the culpability* in the educational relationship. All too often, we let this "you are the guilty one" pattern determine our parental thoughts, our explanations, and even our disciplinary responses. However, we overlook the fact that our children and many adolescents are not yet liable (culpable). They are in the truest sense of the word, "innocent"—but only to the extent that we assign no blame to them. Guilt presupposes responsibility or culpability for an action. Yet, how can we make what we expect in terms of our parenting goals—namely, the development of a responsible mature adult—into a requirement for our children and adolescents who now challenge us? The simple answer is: We cannot! Certainly, children and teenagers should learn to accept responsibility, yet this does not work if we make them feel guilty, but rather, only when we give them access to an external view of their actions. They need to learn to see their actions from the perspective of another and understand what the action means to the other. Accepting responsibility presupposes that you are given an opportunity to put yourself in another person's position and consider what impact your behavior has from their standpoint. This is a cautious and subtle change of perspectives which no one can force, but also cannot be skipped over through some oppressive accusation of blame.

> Never miss an opportunity to encourage your child to change perspective. You know now that the liability for responsible action derives from the ability to feel the impact of your own conduct from the standpoint of another, not from the notion of blame.

EXERCISE: "NO UNLOADING THE BLAME!"

Textbox 25.2

One teacher told me that she had thought of a certain "punishment" for the students involved in excited quarrels and brawls: They are asked to write a brief one-page witness report about the incident, which has to be written from the perspective of their "courtroom opponent." Another important caveat: They can only win the case for their own position in the specific dispute if they are successful in breaking down their "opponent's standpoint" before the "court!" Finally, the students are asked not to use the word "blame" in their statements, but to limit themselves to words that state why the position of "their" opponent is justified, unintentional, or harmless. "It is not easy to motivate students to get involved in this change of perspective. Emotions are running too high and each one has the feeling of being right," explained the teacher. "Sometimes it doesn't work. In that case, the parties must appoint a 'second,' who takes over this job for them. In any case, it is no longer necessary for me to settle the dispute!"

Practice 2-way conversations!

Some years ago, a study commissioned by the United Nations children's organization UNICEF published its conclusion that the climate of discussion between parents and children is very different among the European countries. For example, parents in Italy speak more minutes per day with their children than German parents do and, in doing so, use significantly fewer reproachful or controlling words. European children experience different worlds as they develop. While one may already experience acceptance in the role of a discussion partner and being listened to as a small child, another is made to unmistakably feel that adults usually only speak to them when they disagree with something.

European children grow up in different worlds: one world of unconditional openness ("I talk with you and listen to you simply because you are important to me!") and another of rebuke and control ("I talk with you to tell you what to do!").

REFLECT ON YOUR OWN EDUCATIONAL DISCUSSION STYLE

Observe the nature of your parenting dialogs and ask: "When talking with my children, what percentage of my time is devoted to giving advice, direction, or a reprimand?" Practice the art of inquiring conversation!

If you want to reach out to your children and teenagers and not merely reprimand or even intimidate them, you should make a habit of talking in a way that achieves this. This is not always easy because

Checklist: Reflecting on my educational discussion style		Often	Rarely	Never
	Today, I have …			
Knowing	*… learned or tried to learn something about the wishes, concerns, joys of my children.*			
Revealing	*… shown my child how important he/she is to me (e.g., by devoting my time to them).*			
Inquiring	*… asked with genuine interest what motivates my child.*			
Tolerant	*… signaled my willingness to accept something that seems strange and perhaps even wrong, because it is important to him/her.*			
Accepting	*… recognized, praised, or appreciated something my child has done.*			
Cooperative	*… supported my children or let them know they can always "fall back on me."*			
Trusting	*… communicated to my child that I, as a rule, will trust him/her and I know they can find a solution to their problems.*			

Figure 26.1

communicating with adolescents is a delicate undertaking. Children and teenagers listen with all antennae to what is said and how it is said. They are searching for themselves and pay subtle attention to what resonates back to them from the adult world. And, how quickly they close their ears and hearts when they get the impression they are not understood. Give some thought to the following important principle for your parenting conversation:

> Always ensure that you convey a positive message to show the other person how important it is to you not to let momentary anger damage or even permanently ruin your relationship. It is hard to reopen a heart once it is closed. Consequently, practice defining clear but appreciative boundaries! Meditate over your deeper appreciation for those who have exceeded your limits!

Textbox 26.1

One father mentioned how much his son had changed over the last two years: "When I think about the way he runs around all the time signaling his 'apathetic mood,' I have to say: 'He is really no longer a son of mine!'"

Unknowingly, the father is describing part of a vicious circle, to which youth repeatedly fall victim. In order to differentiate themselves, they have a need for attention and seek confrontation. Most youth develop a strong outward orientation rather than to their own family, but still, this avoidance may be further accelerated by the fact that the opportunities for contact and conversation at home are limited. Parents see themselves, especially, with children in puberty, facing two tasks simultaneously. One is to let go, while the other is to make contact and communicate openly in a way that the searching adolescent will feel accepted and "OK." Both tasks are difficult and frequently, parents are overwhelmed:

- They try to bond with the child by trying to force them to follow *their* expectations and directions. This is usually associated with an escalation of threats and punishments (motto: "As long as you sleep under my roof . . ."), or
- they forfeit the last real opportunity for dialog with the child who is, after all, still their child (motto: "This is no child of mine!").

The pair of failures is quite common and is the cause of many breaks between parents and their children. The feeling solidifies in both of them that it is "the other who is wrong and does not understand me." Once this point is reached, the adult is the one who has the chance to re-establish the contact with their children through a deliberate change of style in the parenting dialog.

You cannot really change the behavior of a child or an adolescent. You can only change the way you respond to the behavior—in particular, if the previous methods employed to deal with it proved less then success-ful. If you change the style of your educational conversation, your child has an opportunity to present himself or herself from a different side.

THE RULES OF CONTACT AND CONDUCT

Consider the following rules of contact and conduct:

Rule	Rating
1. Modify the picture that you carry inside. Meditate for 15 minutes every day about how your child is unique!	
2. Avoid direct confrontation!	
3. Look for situations of silent companionship (e.g., at breakfast, while driving, etc.)!	
4. Take advantage of situations in which your child tells you something by responding with interest and by not judging!	
5. Signal to your child that you like being together and devote time whenever the opportunity arises!	
6. Share your child's concerns, worries, and questions, without giving advice or your own interpretation right away!	
7. Establish or practice common rituals (e.g., have a daily meal together)!	
8. Practice the delayed response, i.e., avoid the known conflict issues and points of contention and postpone your clarifications!	
9. Welcome your child's world (music, fashion, etc.) – even if it is foreign to you!	
10. Notice how similar to you your children are, in finding their own way, in differentiating and defining themselves!	
Each week, on a scale of A (very successful) to C (less successful), evaluate your ability to apply these rules in your daily parenting conversations!	

Figure 26.2

Escape from the self-expectations and enjoy the diversity of the world!

Disciplinary problems are also an oppressive experience for many parents, because they feel responsible and believe that they have "failed." If you feel that you "failed," you may also think that had you only acted "correctly," everything would be different. This form of self-incrimination is understandable, but, in many ways, unjustified. It may also block your ability to see the many other alternative behaviors available to you as a parent.

Textbox 27.1

"I think I have done everything wrong in raising my children," said one mother as we discussed her problems with her children. They had developed entirely different than she had expected. In many ways, they even denied the way of life which the mother herself had lived. "Face the problems in life and master their challenges without any help from others"—this was the motto of her life and also what she expected her children to do. The next few questions point out the dilemma to the mother: "Can you really jump over your own shadow and actually look at your children without any expectations? What would happen if you left the country right now and your children were left to their own devices? Would they get their lives in order then? Could it just be that you expect your children to be independent but, at the same time, expect them to develop the way you want? In other words, remain dependent on you?"

Parents cannot guaranty the success of their parenting effort because children also develop from within. Child rearing is just a framework which gives them room for self-development. In a loving, tolerant, and attentive environment, adolescents find more favorable opportunities to develop what they have inside. There are no fixed if-then laws. Everyone has heard the examples of people accomplishing great things despite all the odds against them and we also know about children who, in spite of having an optimal social upbringing and opportunities, could not find any direction in their lives. This is why the following statement is made:

You are not fully responsible for what becomes of your children, but only partially responsible. Avoid self-accusations ("I have failed" . . .), because that is to assume the feasibility of success that does not exist! If your children "disappoint" you, always ask yourself what criteria you are using to evaluate their behavior and whether those criteria are really theirs too.

The session with the mother took a surprising turn in subsequent meetings. She had stopped seeing her children as "rule breakers" and made a greater effort to reflect on herself and her conflicting messages.

Textbox 27.2

"I must admit, my entire life as a mother was characterized by my narrow view of my children. My message was always something like: 'Live independently, but make me happy!' It is no wonder that they were confused. Either they gave me joy and remained in some way dependent on me, or they tried to become independent and had to turn away from me. I got the feeling from somewhere that it was me causing the imbalance and my children were having a very difficult time with it. It was like a trap for them, which they could not escape without falling back in!"

In coming to this realization, the mother described what is known in communications theory as the "double bind trap." We simultaneously confront the other person with a double expectation. In order to satisfy one of these expectations, they must violate the other. There is no escape—not for the child at whom it is directed, or for the parents who are always presented with the same effect: "My child does not do what I expect!" Nevertheless, communication studies also tell us how to get out of the "double bind trap": Only the one who sets the trap can make this happen, for example, by recognizing the ambiguity of the message given to the child and ending it. This exit takes practice and time. The trap used to capture the other person also serves its purpose. It is precisely this purpose that we often do not want to do without. In this example, the double bind served the mother to face her own fears of being deserted by her children and being left alone. The contradictory messages communicated to the children achieved the "desired" effect: her children kept her busy—even if only through the constant worry about the "non-fulfillment" of a part of the message. The case illustrates:

We are also, unintentionally expressing our deepest fears in the way we communicate with our children. These anxieties mingle time and again with the impressions and the interpretations of their behavior and we reach for conclusions and disciplinary measures that are not only directed at them, but also serve us—without us being aware of the subtle benefit to ourselves.

"How ridiculous"— was the initial reaction of the mother when she heard about this logical effect of her ambiguous parenting style. It took some time for her to come to the insight that, perhaps, she herself was weaving the entanglements that snared her children again and again. Once aware of this, she was able to concentrate more on the "road to clarity" in relationships, and along the way, she also learned to free herself from her own excessive demands.

Many people live entangled lives (Nelles 2010). In other words, they act out of perceived or real expectations and not from their own initiative. They remain loyal and dependent or become harsh and seek conflict, without really understanding what drives them and, sometimes, even leads them to great success. However, their actions are never the result of their own will, but rather serve, in some hidden way, for the fulfillment of the expectations of others. When these people, at some

Table 27.1

The road to clarity
Check to see if you are sending ambiguous messages to your children!
Identify these messages and compare them. Remember situations in which you articulated both at the same time.
Decide on the message—which one is closer to your heart and depart from the other!
This is easier said than done, for the second message is usually a subliminal one that serves its own hidden agenda.
Expose the ambiguous personal need and express it such as it is ("It would do me some good, if you . . .")!
Consider where or with whom you can live out these needs (for togetherness, joy, etc.) and plan an alternative satisfaction of your ego!
Practice signaling to your children, over and over again, what expectations you hold dear regarding their behavior or their aims!
It is always difficult in the beginning to practice being specific and to remain consistent. It may help to use some standard phrase.

point in their lives, have to position themselves, for example, to enter into a sincere relationship with another ("with open eyes") or even when they have children of their own, they may find that they have little to fall back on of themselves. At the latest, that is when the consequences of an upbringing based on entanglement, not on a relationship, start to appear.

Parents have the opportunity to prevent or reduce the entanglements of their children. They can do this by recognizing ambiguous relationship messages and practicing clarity in the relationship. In the process, they make a major contribution to the child's long-term mental health, by helping them at an early stage to discover and develop themselves.

Provide encouragement, avoid disciplining!

This rule is not new; however, it is rarely followed. Parents and teachers have a tendency to take "normal conduct" of their children or students for granted and focus instead on the deviant behaviors. This narrow view of adolescent behavior results in controls and reprimands—the things of which education is still made. Shielding is also a form of control. If you shield your child, you run the risk of taking away an opportunity for self-development. This happens with the best of intentions since educational responsibility also consists of watching over your children and protecting them from harm.

Effective parenting saps energy. This is generated from feelings of encouragement and trust, not controls and reprimands. Only when your children feel that you are on their side and that you will appreciate them regardless of outcome, can they develop the inner strength and confidence that makes them strong.

Checklist: Determine the extent of encouragement in your parenting style In the last three weeks, have you	Rarely	Sometimes	Often
... praised your children several times?			
... shown them that you believe in them and have trust in them?			
... stood by them in times of doubt and disappointment?			
... assigned them a task of responsibility (without controlling them)?			
... taught them that you can learn from mistakes and failures?			
... felt that something is wrong and tried to talk with them?			
... provided them comfort and encouragement?			
... defended them?			
Complete every question. Each field answered with "rarely" indicates an area in which your style should be more encouraging.			

Figure 28.1

The long-term effects of humiliation and control are often devastating to the development of a child, as Franz Kafka, at age 36, wrote in his "Dearest Father" letter:

> There is only one episode in the early years of which I have a direct memory. You may remember it, too. One night, I kept on whimpering for water, not, I am certain, because I was thirsty, but probably partly to be annoying, partly to amuse myself. After several vigorous threats had failed to have any effect, you took me out of bed, carried me out onto the pavlatche, and left me there alone for a while in my nightshirt, outside the shut door. I am not going to say that this was wrong—perhaps there was really no other way of getting peace and quiet that night—but I mention it as typical of your methods of bringing up a child and their effect on me. I dare say I was quite obedient afterward at that period, but it did me inner harm. What was for me a matter of course, that senseless asking for water, and then the extraordinary terror of being carried outside were two things that I, my nature being what it was, could never properly connect with each other. Even years afterward I suffered from the tormenting fancy that the huge man, my father, the ultimate authority, would come almost for no reason at all and take me out of bed in the night and carry me out onto the pavlatche, and that consequently I meant absolutely nothing as far as he was concerned.
>
> That was only a small beginning, but this feeling of being nothing that often dominates me (a feeling that is in another respect, admittedly, also a noble and fruitful one) comes largely from your influence. What I would have needed was a little encouragement, a little friendliness, a little keeping open of my road, instead of which you blocked it for me, though of course with the good intention of making me take another road. But I was not fit for that. (Kafka 1999, p. 9)

This autobiographical reflection shows in an extreme fashion the scars that may be inflicted through parenting. Their effects cannot be limited and what may initially appear as unimportant measures can, in fact, last a lifetime. Years later, the 36-year-old penned this memory of a key experience, in which a feeling of helplessness against unbridled authority was branded into him and his words still show a noticeable bowing of the head. It is a steep slope that Kafka is describing—a slope of intimidation and control, lacking all encouragement and appreciation:

In any case, we were so different and in our difference so dangerous to each other that if anyone had tried to calculate in advance how I, the slowly developing child, and you, the full-grown man, would behave toward one another, he could have assumed that you would simply trample me underfoot so that nothing was left of me. (ibid., p. 8)

In these descriptions, we encounter a frequently cited element of education, namely, "parental authority." This assumes that the weaker must obey the stronger, without questioning the authority of the stronger. This way of thinking is a holdover from the past, in which the "need to be educated" is at the heart of the matter: at the start of their development, people—according to the theory—are an "unfinished product" in need of a model, a guiding hand as well as the experience of the elders—that is, "parents!" to prepare them for their roles as responsible adults. This claim is not without problems. What is proposed as a kind of natural law, that can be used for anything—even disciplining the upcoming generation for the sake of discipline—should not go unquestioned. If you favor this discipline, you must also say something of the historical situation in which the Germans turned discipline into a higher art form.

It all went like "clockwork" in the schools, on the parade fields, but also in the concentration camps. Those being disciplined are muzzled. Those subjected to punishment act not out of conviction. Discipline without the self leads to alienation from the self. The result is a person that mechanically learns rules and provisions, who subscribes to blind acceptance of authority and discipline, and is truly unable to have a loving relationship with another (Bueb 2006, p. 11). They have not learned how to ask the purpose or question the authority for what they are doing or what they are told to do. (Arnold 2007)

But, is this what we want?—This "blind acceptance of authority and discipline" (Bueb 2006, p. 11) as the tabloid press and popular self-help literature would have us believe? Is it not rather the "caveats" that provide the freedoms, the courage, and even the solidarity of man? Do we not need "In Praise of Provisos?" Was it not the guardians of the German virtue of discipline who did nothing to oppose the historical brutality, but rather, enthusiastically assisted in its design? In the light of this historical legacy, can cheering for more discipline really be justified without even giving serious thought to the fact that there was a time when a collective ability to choose a lack of discipline would have allowed us to walk upright? It is the hallmark of democratic societies to cultivate "provisos" and not "discipline."

Avoid discipline for discipline's sake. It teaches the individual a formal principle, probably for the sake of peace in the living room or on the playground, and actually, does not seriously care about what happens to the child, his resistance, rebelliousness, and willingness to fight—all character traits or even "virtues" that a vibrant democratic society cannot be without.

Avoid overreaction or apologize for it!

Some principles are simply followed and are rarely questioned by parents and teachers. One of these principles states: "Never show weakness. You cannot lose your face; otherwise you will lose the respect of the children and adolescents!" Perhaps, this is the reason why, once your decision is made, you stand by it and stay firm. Of course, knowing the consequence is a major prerequisite if the child is to take you seriously and perceive you as predictable. Yet, this does not apply for a consequence just for consequence sake. If parents or teachers are mistaken, or are overreacting, and, despite this, still adhere to their original decision, they are being stubborn, not consequent.

Review your parenting response and avoid intractability: Consequences for the sake of being consequential are not educationally effective. They destroy confidence in the justice of what you expect from the children and adolescents.

Textbox 29.1

One high school teacher found himself unable to continue due to the permanent noise and lack of concentration in his classroom. At first, he attempted to get the class "back under control" in his words, using the occasional punishment. When that did not work, he told all of his students to take out a sheet of paper and complete an unannounced quiz. He then announced: "This quiz counts as one of the four graded exercises included in the calculation of your oral grades for the year"—in itself a rather illogical connection. Grudgingly, but finally with the necessary quiet, the students acquiesced because

(cont...)

Textbox 29.1 *(cont...)*

> the fear of a poor grade gave credibility to the disciplinary measure. The teacher corrected the quizzes and the next day assigned grades of D's and F's (deficient and failing) to two thirds of the students in his class. The best grade was a C. In one of the many discussions that followed between the teacher and some angry parents, one father surprised the teacher with the comment: "I can understand you. The same thing always happens to me. Out of anger and disappointment, I also react with some disciplinary measure that is actually in effect wrong. But then I go apologize to my children! That is what you need to do now. That is the only way students will learn about fairness and justice, but also about being human. To experience the fact that we can make mistakes and admit them is one of the most important lessons in growing up!"

Overreactions are not educational measures, although they undermine all of us every now and then. This is understandable. Sometimes we find ourselves in situations that overwhelm us and we do not know how to create "peace and quiet" or deal with unreasonableness. "That's the last straw!" or "My patience is at an end!" is an inner statement with which we like to justify our behavior. It is not easy for us to note without emotion, namely, "Now there is no chance for me to enter into a constructive cooperation with them. Something has closed all the access doors!" By then, good advice is hard to come by and something inside of us is reluctant to abandon our plan and try something else— a game, a joint activity, or something similar. Effective education demands:

> If you notice that something is not working, try something else—without any annoyance or inner reproach!

Textbox 29.2

> One teacher reported: "When my class simply refuses to pay attention, I have made a good experience with an exercise called the

(cont...)

Textbox 29.2 *(cont...)*

'Observer Game.' I silently approach several of the students who are not too involved in the offending hustle and bustle, and invite them to form so-called observer groups (always 3–5 students) while the disturbance in the class continues. Sometimes, the restlessness already starts to subside as I post these groups around the periphery of the class. Usually, there is one group of 'referees,' a group of 'sports reporters,' and one for 'scouts.' They simply have to observe what is happening, although my students already know what it is all about." In this spontaneous exercise, each group has three questions, through which they observe the events.

Referees
What is the score? (Who is winning?)
Who are the game makers?
What violations of the rules have taken place?

Sports reporters
What are the highlights of the match?
How are the players doing?
Who is the "Hero of the match"?

Scouts
Who do we want to acquire?
Who are the strong players?
What positions (offense, defense, etc.)?

Often, this playful exercise alone is enough to get the attention of the class. If someone feels they are being watched, their behavior changes—that is what I have found out. If things have quieted down the groups have the opportunity to briefly speak about what is happening and, in the perfect case, the entire class listens to these discussions. I have heard match reports that include very specific feedback. The students are sometimes surprisingly different in the perceptions and candid in their comments.

Again, this report shows that in situations where you do not know what to do, it is senseless to continue with what has already been tried, for example, to re-establish order. It is far better to try something else. Parents and educators who are finally trying to make themselves heard are nearly always involved in a cycle of escalation: They repeat their instructions, become loud, and sometimes react out of anger and disappointment or resort to Draconian measures. As one student said to his neighbor, "He is freaking out again!" This comment shows that the boundary between obstinate and ridiculous in the eyes of the child is often fluid and there is a point beyond which they can no longer take us seriously. To avoid this point, it does not help to invoke the "authority of office" and demand a "blind acceptance of authority and discipline" (Bueb 2007, p. 11). Such requirements do not help parents or teachers who have reached their wit's end. Yet, we repeatedly find ourselves deciding for drastic measures—supported by the illusion that something is to be gained by pushing through our expectations with threats and punishments, without noticing that we are losing our contact with the children and adolescents precisely as a result of this stubbornness. Sometimes, it is necessary that we admit that it is simply a matter of our own principles, that is, our roles as fathers, mothers, and teachers.

Textbox 29.3

After his meeting with the parents, it was clear to the high school teacher that his overreaction was like an elephant in a porcelain shop. A few days later, he addressed the class with the following words: "Listen up, I have been thinking about my reaction to the situation last Tuesday, when I gave you the unannounced quiz that resulted in so many poor grades. I have to admit that I was very angry and frustrated and did not know what else to do. My job is to provide you with a reasonably good education, but there are times when that does not work. Last Tuesday was one of those times. My reaction to the situation was wrong and I used the performance test as a disciplinary tool. I apologize for that and I take it back. I will not include those grades in your end of year grades. I have resolved to react differently in similar situations in the future." Contrary to expectations, the students did not judge this admission as a sign of weakness, but rather knew, "here is a teacher who can admit mistakes and correct them."

The way out of the parenting doldrums

We could thereby avoid,
"(. . .) every generation having to start over
and doing things that have been done before."

(Schleiermacher 1959, p. 11)

Yes, they do exist: the "well-mannered children." It is by no means universal that they all come from orderly relationships and, vice versa, such orderly relationships are by no means a guaranty that the developing child knows "what belongs and what does not." But then what does "belong?" The more we think about it, the more fragile our image becomes. Certainly today, in the various countries of the world, there is still a common sense of what behavior is considered reasonable, and in nearly every culture, the respect of the elder by the younger is a consistent pattern. Although, the answers to the question of how to express this respect and what conduct to consider as improper are very different. In modern societies, these ideas fundamentally change over the course of time: The expectations that were valid yesterday are no longer valid today, and what is a legitimate concept can already be empty and in the dust bin tomorrow.

It is true that education without values is like a body without blood: anemic.

Values and moral concepts give people direction. Values provide meaning. They are an expression of the emotions and individual soul, by which we know ourselves, but also have a connection with other—like-minded—people. We are steeped in values; they are the basis of our convictions. Values cause us to have an understanding of life. For this reason, in modern societies, people sometimes fall into a peculiar helplessness and inner emptiness as the supply of commonly shared—binding—values shrinks. We live in a pluralistic society as the social scientists say. The influences of church and government, fortunately, no longer press the individual into a biographical corset, in which there is never any need to ask what is allowed and what is not. In earlier societies, if someone deviated from the values, perhaps to seek a better life, they were often persecuted, expelled, or even killed. The only concept of life and community that applied to the individual and the children was the one of authority: It was a value-controlled society, not a pluralistic—free—community. The concept of the individual could not be freely expressed; the effective values were ones of adoption and subordination, not those of self-determination.

This changed with the liberation movements of the nineteenth century, when people began to risk their lives to create a society in which a lifestyle that includes the freedoms of self-determination and solidarity is possible: a democracy. The mood is expressed in the words of this folksong of the times (1848 Revolution):

If we wear red or yellow collars,
Whether helmets or hats,
Boots or shoes;
Or, if we sew the coats
And make the wire for the shoes,
That matters not.
(. . .)
But if we build the new,
Or just digest the old,
Like cows chewing grass;
If we create something in this world,
Or, just watch it go by,
That matters, that does matter.

If we are active and industrious,
And where strength is needed
Always brave and reaching for it;
Or if we lazily think:

"God will provide it while we sleep,"
That matters, that does matter!

(Stern 1974, p. 83f)

This song shows what it is all about. The central idea was to establish a future of active and safe cooperation among equals ("whether
helmets or hats")—an attitude also expressed in "the American Dream"
(Postman). This is a value concept, in which the right to individual
happiness is firmly anchored. All persons in this new world—all skin
colors, all religions, gender neutral—are seen as equals. And, with this
right, education is an obligation above all else. This is the foundation of
humanistic education. It provides a framework that the rules of human
cooperation cannot ignore.

If you cannot teach values, if they can only be lived and experienced,
parents and educators must ask: "What? That cannot be it. There must
be more!" At first, that is all. No evidence from educational research
exists to indicate that adolescents suddenly change their behavior, just
because, along the way, someone gives them a maxim for life. Whether,
and to what extent, they follow the encountered values is left solely up to
them—as painful as that insight might be to the educational experts. Nevertheless, there is consolation from another—perhaps unexpected—side:

*People, as a rule, practice a value-related, value-based behavior, if they
have experienced their own value in respectful social interactions.*

This indicates that although no direct teaching occurs, an indirect
formation of values is possible. Although no direct teaching occurs,
an indirect formation of values is possible. If parents and educators
are able to treat children and adolescents in more than a directing and
controlling way, the child will have a greater chance of being prepared
to relive the experience in their own dealings with people.

If your children annoy you, if their behavior disappoints you and you
are sometimes shocked, then you usually react without thinking, often
feeling irritated and a need for dominance. Children also get the brunt
of your frustrations—after a hard day at work or after an unsuccessful
attempt as a teacher, to finally begin with the classroom instruction.
Whenever you have a "gut reaction" and, in your reactions, have only

expectations of others, you will find yourself stuck in the world of ineffective education. In that case, education has more the character of an outraged adult than the prudent and deliberate promotion of self-respect and value formation.

When can we react in the sense of prudent and deliberate? Take a minute for the self-evaluation below to find out how good you really are as a teacher:

Table E1

Am I a good teacher?
How you can promote self-respect and value formation

Self

1. I focus on the others, observing reactions and behavior in a loving way, and generally have appreciative reaction ("without looking at the individual"). — *. . . Fairness and kindness are not just "preached," but lived.*

2. I seek conversation and listen to the descriptions and depictions ("as if researching a primitive tribe"). — *. . . Experience self-efficiency as a feeling and it can lead to self-respect.*

3. I am aware of my own sensitivities and tame my ill-tempered and disappointed reactions. — *. . . Self-control and individual reserve are experienced.*

Facts

4. The subject is important, but is not what matters at the core. What matters are the students and their development. — *. . . I strengthen the other's feeling of "I am important!"*

5. I never tire of repeatedly explaining technical issues: I am an advisor and counselor, not a censor or even a selector. — *. . . Patience and the mastery of emotions (like disappointment) can be experienced.*

6. I explain and listen: the subject loses its threatening nature and becomes an issue for all. — *. . . The content loses its crushing effect and self-confidence increases.*

We

7. I take care of the group cohesion and the development of a "we-feeling." — *. . . The importance of a social and supportive attitude is experienced.*

8. I do not tolerate laughing at another's misfortune and disrespectful behavior; rather, I always encourage cooperation and solidarity. — *. . . I ignore/stop destructive attitudes through social values and concepts.*

9. I pay special attention to the outsiders and losers and show them (and the others) their unique talents. — *. . . I enable the experience of supporting the individual.*

"Discipline" alone is not able to provide a framework for education.

What teacher does not wish for a group of concentrated and well-disciplined students who, perhaps even enthusiastically, are "into the subject"? However, start to imagine what things would be like in such a class and the images that come to mind are those from the nineteenth century or early twentieth century. Such images actually exist. They pictured uniformed children, arranged in rows, listening to the instruction with hands folded on the desk. They correspond exactly with what is expected, and any deviation from this is met with severe punishment. The educational atmosphere created in this way is somewhat militaristic in nature: this is a world of commands and obedience, in which individual thought, creativity, and development has little chance.

As parents and teachers, we are generally proficient. Most are able to identify the cause of problems and we also agree that education has never been so difficult and the problems in motivating children and adolescents to cooperate have never been so bad.

Textbox E1

"Today was another one of those days!"—complained the young teacher as she got home. "They drove me over the edge again. Daniel is the worst of all of them. He can rattle the whole class, and then you can forget about teaching anything." Her husband, who is more than familiar with these "reports from the front," as he likes to calls them, sympathetically asked: "What really happened this time?" Exhausted, the teacher collapsed into the sofa and with tears in her eyes, said: "Three times, yes, three times I tried to introduce the subject and each time . . ."—she let her hand fall into her lap with an exhausted gesture—". . . each time he blurted out something in class. Here and there came some laughter and it was clear they were listening more to him than to what I was trying to teach. Finally, I didn't know what else to do and I screamed at him and sent him out the door. I am so frustrated I can't even begin!" Her husband sat down next to her and tried to comfort her: "But he is just one student, one of 23 that you have to deal with. Try talking

(cont...)

Textbox E1 *(cont...)*

> to his parents again."—"You're good. What do you think I have already done four times? His mother and even his father—I have talked to both. They themselves do not know what to do! Do you know what they told me? Their darling little angel won't let anyone say anything to him. He does or doesn't do whatever he wants; even house arrest does not do any good. He simply ignores the rules and goes out anyway. As they tried to take away his allowance he said, 'OK, I'll just steal the things I need.' Of course they don't want that to happen either. I just don't know anymore. I am really afraid of the next class with him. . ."

Such descriptions are common when talking to teachers. Even parents have similar stories. As helplessness and despair come to dominate, self-help manuals sell very well. They promise solutions to the problem, mainly in the form of old slogans: "Set clear limits!" "Demand respect!" "We need more courage and moral values in education." Also, the comfortable school assignments are widely used and always justified with "In the old days, things were so much better" which, in retrospective, is not true. The familiar complaint was first noted by Socrates (470–399 v. Chr.) and reads as follows:

> Our youth now love luxury. They have bad manners, contempt for authority; they show disrespect for their elders and love chatter in place of exercise; they no longer rise when elders enter the room; they contradict their parents, chatter before company; gobble up their food and tyrannize their teachers.[1]

They have always been there: the tyrannical children or, at least, the idea that they were there, which brings up the question of "why are our children such tyrants" (Winterhoff 2009). Although always an interesting question, it is not really new and useful. If you see your child as a tyrant you have already, in effect, closed your access to them. You cannot teach a tyrant, only overthrow them—an insight that clearly shows us how self-help guides lead us astray. Today, they tell us that the new media, or the fragile family relationships, are to blame for the fact that education is so much more difficult now than in earlier times. Or, it is the aftereffects of the flower-power generation that are responsible for the fact that authority and obedience no longer hold any resonance. All these arguments have one thing in common: They are beyond your reach. You cannot really influence them, which is why they are only able to explain their own ineffectiveness. They are not able to contribute any useful perspectives for parents and teachers on what can be done. These are placebos that do not require a prescription. They convey an illusion of healing, but provide none.

I call such placebos "parenting laments," which can help you endure, but can also become an entanglement. You should know that to endure only weakens and does not strengthen. If you argue along these lines, or follow such guides, you will not find any new starting points for a potentially more effective way to deal with your children or students. Nevertheless, you can always lean back on your ineffectiveness in comfort without any feelings of guilt because you are the victim of a darker force responsible for the misery. You find understanding every-where, perhaps even sympathy. Frequently, one of these self-laments leads to giving up and your inner surrender. For we also reach for these self-help guides in order to justify our own failures to ourselves and others, again and again.

Distrust all self-help guides that pack all educational issues into a wider context (such as "loss of values," "today's family relationships," "computers and media"). By following such laments, you will achieve just one thing: you will perceive yourself as the victim of adverse circumstances. But, did you know that you cannot be a good parent as a victim? Victims see their children as offenders. And, if you are an offender (or feel like an offender), you will turn your back on the relationship.

THE BASIS OF ALL EFFECTIVE EDUCATION IS THE RELATIONSHIP

As parents and teachers we cannot give up, and we do not have to either. What we need along with a good portion of realism is to say good-bye to parenting laments of any kind. Educational researchers have given us a good tip concerning the latter: "Parenting is difficult.

It has always been so" (Arnold 2008, p. 12). You can escape from the parenting laments—but to do so, you have to choose to look for realism. This reveals new kinds of access. Although always a difficult thing to do, as long as we accept educating our children as a necessity we can begin our search for truly effective, modern child rearing methods. They do exist. They are more homeopathic than pharmaceutical in nature, sometimes they expect a great deal from us and "we find them hard to swallow." But these are usually the ones that are able to help if we can only try them. Ultimately, it is a solution cocktail that we have to choke down in order to achieve (re-gain) our educational effectiveness—admittedly, a rather extreme image, but effective.

TAKE A PINCH OF PARENTAL PRESENCE

We cannot close our eyes and we cannot withdraw dumb and disappointed, for educational responsibility cannot be rejected or delegated—by parents or by teachers. By demonstrating a presence, we acknowledge our responsibility for the child or the student, even if we do not know (anymore) what it is we should do. This responsibility is the only thing our children have to be "made to feel" if education is to find resonance. This experience is less confrontational than it sounds. It does not express itself in a controlling or reproachful action, but rather as a gesture that clearly explains the attitude of those responsible for educating.

"Whatever happens, I am at your side and I will always be there for you!"—That is the central message of a parenting presence (see Omer/von Schlippe 2005). Numerous problems in education are expressions of what is sometimes an "extreme" search for boundaries. One will not obey his father because he is often away or just never there for the youngster. Another commits acts of violence directed towards the siblings or even the parents—both extreme behaviors that cannot be tolerated. However, you should not simply react without knowing if this behavior is somehow enabling what is buried deep down in his soul. Parents often react with determination to such situations, sometimes also excessively, that is, they react immediately and overdo it. Consequently, they fall into the "escalation trap" explained by Haim Omer and Arist von Schlippe (ibid.): The swift response is experienced as rejection and can therefore lead children to retreat even further and struggle in even more encrypted ways, to find themselves and the limiting parental presence.

NOTE

1. This quote is attributed to Socrates and has been reprinted many times. This formulation was taken from the Internet (http://english.stackexchange. com/questions/151829/ancient-greek-philosophy-looking-for-a-quotation-of-the-kind-i-am-scared-for). In all probability, it is a free translation from statements in Plato's book *The Republic*, by an anonymous source that can no longer be reconstructed.

References

Andexlinger, H./ Meinen, A.: Denkfragen statt Lenkfragen. In: Lernende Organisation. Zeitschrift für systemisches Management und Organisation, 56 (July/August 2010), pp. 1516–17.

Arnold, R.: Aberglaube Disziplin. Antworten der Pädagogik auf das "Lob der Disziplin." Heidelberg 2007.

Arnold, R. (Hrsg.): Veränderung durch Selbstveränderung. Impulse für ein erfolgreiches Changemanagement. Baltmannsweiler 2010.

Bennack, J.: Erziehungskonzepte in der Schule. Praxishilfen für den Umgang mit Schülerinnen und Schülern. 2. Auflage. Weinheim 2006.

Brunner-Peindl, A.: The non-trivial questioning machine. In: Lernende Organisation. Zeitschrift für systemisches Management und Organisation, 56 (July/August 2010), pp. 1516–17.

Buber, M.: Reden über Erziehung. Heidelberg 1986.

Callo, C.: Modelle des Erziehungsbegriffs. Einführung in pädagogisches Denken. München/ Wien 2002.

Dreikurs, R./ Blumenthal, E.: Wie Parents besser werden. Die häufigsten Erziehungsfehler und ihre Lösungen. Stuttgart 2010.

Fromm, E.: *Die Kunst des Liebens*. München 2000.

Gordon, T.: Lehrer-Schüler-Konferenz. Wie man Konflikte in der Schule löst. 8. Auflage. Munich 1991.

Hennig, C./ Knödler, U.: Schulprobleme lösen. Ein Handbuch für die systemische Beratung. Weinheim/ Basel 2000.

Jacobson, O.: Ich stehe nicht mehr zur Verfügung. Wie sie sich von belastenden Gefühlen befreien und Beziehungen neu erleben. 9th edition. Oberstdorf 2009.

Juul, J.: Aus Erziehung wird Beziehung. Authentische Parents—kompetente Kinder. Freiburg 2005.

Kafka, F.: Brief an den Vater. Frankfurt 1999.

Kindl-Beilfuß, C.: Fragen können wie Küsse schmecken. Systemische Frag-
etechniken für Anfänger und Fortgeschrittene. Heidelberg 2008.

Kreter, G.: Jetzt reicht's: Schüler brauchen Erziehung! Schüler brauchen Erziehung! Was die neuen Kinder nicht mehr können—und was in der Schule
zu tun ist. Seelze-Velber 2001.

Nelles, W.: "Die Gans ist raus"—oder: In der Wirklichkeit gibt es keine Ver-
strickungen. In: Praxis der Systemaufstellungen, 1/2010, pp. 15–29.

Omer, H./ von Schlippe, A.: Autorität durch Beziehung. Die Praxis des
gewaltlosen Widerstandes in der Erziehung. Göttingen 2005.

Omer, H./ von Schlippe, A.v.: Autorität ohne Gewalt. Coaching für Parents
von Kindern mit Verhaltensproblemen. >Elterliche Präsenz< als systemisches Konzept. Göttingen 2006.

Pfeiffer, D.: Klick … Wie moderne Medien uns klüger machen. Frankfurt
2007.

Rotthaus, W.: Wozu erziehen? Entwurf einer systemischen Erziehung.
Heidelberg 2002.

Schleiermacher, F.: Vorlesungen aus dem Jahre 1826. Pädagogische Schriften
I. Frankfurt 1959.

Stern, A.: Lieder gegen den Tritt. Politische Lieder aus fünf Jahrhunderten.
2nd optimized edition. Oberhausen 1974.

Weikert, A.: Tyrannen in Turnschuhen. Überlebensstrategien für geplagte
Eltern. Genf 1994.

Winterhoff, M.: Warum unsere Kinder Tyrannen werden. Oder: Die Abschaf-
fung der Kindheit. 19th edition. Gütersloh 2009.

Wittgenstein, L.: Bemerkungen über die Grundlagen der Mathematik. Oxford
1956.